# THE FACEBOOK NARCISSIST

How to Identify
and Protect Yourself
and Your Loved Ones
from Social Media
Narcissism

## LENA DERHALLY

### Foreword by Mika Brzezinski

Health Communications, Inc.
Boca Raton, Florida
*www.hcibooks.com*

**Disclaimer:** All people in the case studies in this book have had their names, identifying information, and details altered or changed. The author is not diagnosing anyone with narcissistic personality disorder, or any other personality disorder in this book. Narcissism is all on a spectrum and the book is intended to identify and understand narcissistic traits that may present on social media. Narcissistic traits and/or behaviors detailed in this book do not mean that someone has a personality disorder. People often become concerned that they might be a narcissist when they read information on narcissism. The good news is, if you are asking yourself that question, you most likely are not! The word "narcissism" or "narcissist" obviously has a negative connotation, but it is only problematic when it becomes disordered, interferes in the person's functioning and life, and causes harm to others, interpersonally or otherwise.

Library of Congress Cataloging-in-Publication Data
is available through the Library of Congress

© 2022 Lena Derhally

ISBN-13: 978-07573-2429-1 (Paperback)
ISBN-10: 07573-2429-0  (Paperback)
ISBN-13: 978-07573-2430-7 (ePub)
ISBN-10: 07573-2430-4 (ePub)

All rights reserved. Printed in the United States of America. No part of this publication may be reproduced, stored in a retrieval system, or transmitted in any form or by any means, electronic, mechanical, photocopying, recording, or otherwise, without the written permission of the publisher.

HCI, its logos, and marks are trademarks of Health Communications, Inc.

Publisher: Health Communications, Inc.
        1700 NW 2nd Avenue
        Boca Raton, FL 33432-1653

*Cover and Interior design and formatting by Larissa Hise Henoch*

To my dear friend, Lisa McCluskey,
who maintains my website and Facebook
author page so I can keep a healthy distance
from social media—I appreciate all of it.
Love you!

# CONTENTS

# FOREWORD

In *The Facebook Narcissist,* Lena Derhally helps you gain insight into narcissistic behaviors and outlines a way to break through the minefield of social media. Further, providing the tools for you to develop a healthier, functioning relationship with yourself. The narrative in these pages provides an in-depth exploration that you can easily apply to your own experiences.

It will come as no surprise to anyone that prioritizing mental health is a focus and priority of mine. Every day, we're bombarded with depictions of the beautiful, successful, perfect-bodied, socially conscious, and extroverted individuals that our culture has decided is the ideal self, and we berate ourselves when we don't measure up. Social media has changed the world in massive and still poorly understood ways. And narcissism has played an important role in this process at the individual, network, and cultural levels. The guidance in this book can help every single one of us to navigate difficult and challenging times and to thrive.

—**Mika Brzezinski,** co-host of MSNBC's *Morning Joe,*
*New York Times* bestselling author of *Know Your*
*Value, Earn It,* and *Comeback Careers*

# ACKNOWLEDGMENTS

The concept of this book materialized during the COVID-19 pandemic in 2020, with the first full draft written in the first half of 2021 while my children were in a mix of virtual and hybrid school. I was simultaneously trying to see clients in my psychotherapy practice, manage my children's schooling, coach rec soccer, and write a book, among other things. It was an ambitious plan, and at times I really felt like I was crazy, but I was determined to see this concept come to fruition. I am so grateful it did, and this book would never have been possible without the following people:

First and foremost, I have an immense amount of gratitude for my literary agent, **Linda Konner.** There would be no The Facebook Narcissist without her. Linda believed in me right away, and she helped hone this concept to something different than what I had originally presented to her, so the idea was really all hers. Linda, I am forever grateful to you for your guidance, wisdom, and tenacity. This book is out in the world because of you.

I would also like to thank everyone at my publisher, **HCI Books.** The team at HCI has fully supported and embraced my writing as a relatively new author and have included me in the creative process every step of the way. I would especially like to thank my fantastic editor, **Christine Belleris,** who has a real talent for writing catchy subheadings and making a manuscript come alive. Thank you to **Lindsey Mach** for working many months ahead on marketing and publicity. I appreciate all the brainstorming, phone calls, and your dedication to this project!

To **Mika Brzezinski:** You are an inimitable powerhouse, and I am so honored you wrote the foreword for this book. You are the perfect person to help shed light on this important topic. Thank you for all you do. And to **Mark Brzezinski:** Thank you for being a wonderful friend to my family. You are such a positive light in the world, and we are blessed to know you.

I would also like to thank the brilliant and generous experts I interviewed who shared their time, research, and knowledge with me: **W. Keith Campbell, Agnieszka Golec de Zavala, Anne Manne,** and **Kaitlin Ugolik Phillips.** Your work is making the world a better place, and I am truly honored you and your work were a part of this book.

**Hayla Wong** and **Terra Kater,** thank you for generously sharing your stories and your vulnerability for this book. Thank you for all the good you do in the world, and for using social media as a vehicle for positive change.

To all who shared their anonymous stories with me about their experiences with people with narcissistic traits: I know it isn't easy to think about these painful or upsetting experiences, but I also know others reading about your stories (or your loved one's stories) and the survival of narcissistic abuse will help others.

To **1455 Literary Arts,** especially **Sean Murphy** and **Pamela Sorensen,** thank you for your unwavering support of writers and creatives, and thank you so much for your support for me. It means the world.

What helped keep me sane while writing this book was the support of my loved ones. I am lucky to have fantastic friends, but I would in particular like to thank those who were a huge part of support for this particular book over the past two years . . . whether it was sending me surprise donuts, doing group Zoom calls, picking up the phone in my moment of need, having heart to hearts, sharing enthusiasm for this book, reading over the proposal or chapters, and providing feedback for any decision related to the book, I appreciate it all: **Robyn, Jenny HLP, Suz, Christine, Kathryn, Meg, Kim, Erin, Sarah H, Massi, Meredith,** and **Kasia.**

This book is dedicated to one of my dearest friends, **Lisa McCluskey,** but she also belongs here in the acknowledgments. Lisa is not only a caring friend, but she has been handling my marketing, social media, and website since I became an author in 2019. I am so grateful for all you do, and words will never adequately express my gratitude. I hope surprise cases of Diet Coke and Vietnamese coffee are just some of the ways you know how appreciated you are.

My good friends **Amanda** and **Kerstin** deserve an award for being the most generous friends a gal could ask for. They have been there for me every day, always available to video chat. They have been through every single up and down, providing feedback, support, and generally just being my biggest cheerleaders. I don't know what I would have done without either of you throughout this process, and in general. I have so much gratitude and love for you both.

I am also incredibly lucky to have a supportive family, including a large extended family. Thank you for all the support and love to my siblings (this includes my amazing siblings-in-law), my uncles, aunts, cousins, and my cousins-in-law.

Most importantly in the family, my parents, **Candace** and **Odeh** are my biggest fans. Their belief and unconditional love for me is truly why I have been able to pursue my dreams in life. Thank you for modeling persistence, love, confidence, compassion, generosity, and integrity for me.

My children are my biggest inspiration and are the most compassionate, inclusive, and generous humans I know. In a world that can often seem cruel and unforgiving, they remind me of all that is good.

Last but certainly not least, this book would certainly not have been possible without my husband, **Zeid.** He supports all my ideas, dreams, and most importantly my happiness. He is a true partner in every sense of the word and my best friend and biggest supporter. Thank you for always being in my corner and for helping to make all the dreams I had as a little girl come true.

Throughout the twenty years I had his physical presence with me, my **Grandpa Felix** used to always say: *"Lena never gives up!"* Whenever things seem insurmountable, I still hear him saying that to me. I miss him every day. Grandpa Felix, this book is for you.

# Introduction:

# THE ALARMING LINKS BETWEEN NARCISSISM AND SOCIAL MEDIA

## June: The Entitled Mommy Blogger

It all started out innocently enough. June had always secretly wanted to be famous, although she would never publicly admit that. She met her husband Michael after completing college, and soon after getting married, they settled down in the suburbs and started a family. June had dreams of becoming a model but never pursued that career. June, now a stay-at-home mother, spent hours scrolling through Instagram, following bloggers with babies and young children. It felt good to relate to others who were in a similar life stage. Many of June's friends did not have children yet, and she felt what many new mothers often do—isolated and navigating a new lifestyle.

As June continued to scroll through the glossy, filtered photos of Instagram, she thought that she could be a blogger, too, and so that is what she became when her first child turned one. To her surprise, when she started her own Instagram page, she started to gain followers rather quickly.

As much as she initially set out to portray authenticity—the good, the bad, and the ugly of motherhood—she realized all her pictures would need to be aesthetically beautiful and highly filtered if she were to succeed at becoming an Instagram influencer. June would wake up every morning and spend at least an hour doing her makeup and hair. She also began to work out obsessively and take live videos of her workouts, talking to her followers while primping and preening for the camera.

June was always a bit superficial, but blogging, which started out as a hobby, became an addiction and she grew obsessive about her appearance. She was hooked on the feeling that came with the validation from thousands of "likes" on her posts, and now national brands were starting to ask her to promote their products. This all made her feel famous and important, which is what she always wanted. June finally felt, after many years of secretly harboring the desire for someone to "discover" her and make her famous, that people were recognizing her for how special she was. Even more intoxicating to her was that she was able to monetize her personal brand by posting photos of the everyday minutiae of her life.

This self-styled influencer felt she could not say no to any brand that asked her to promote their product because now she was getting paid; being a mommy blogger and influencer was now her career path. The more she became addicted to the feelings of validation, the more time she spent curating her life as opposed to just living it. She loved boasting about how many followers she had and loved talking about her perceived success.

June's young children were forced into constantly posing for staged pictures, often multiple times a day. When June had to promote a brand, her husband and children would often be part of the photo shoot. She would stage artificial family meals, outings, and interactions. Her phone's video camera was constantly at the ready, as she regularly whipped it out to record every aspect of her life that she would later filter and post.

Sometimes, she would take hundreds of photos just to find the perfect one for Instagram. What started out as a blog ended up a vanity project, where the focus of her family became about the perfect pictures, money, and a mostly false image of an attractive couple, living in a beautiful home, with the perfect children. Sadly, June's children became innocent victims of her narcissism, which was further exacerbated by her constant social media use. Although she couldn't see it, her children were merely props to her, and their wants, needs, and feelings were never considered. To some social media-savvy users, her husband could also be known as the infamous "Instagram husband"—not only was he taking all the photographs, but he also went along with whatever June wanted.

Although June was savvy enough to know that her personal and polarizing worldviews would not be appropriate for her blog, she secretly held many entitled, racist, and prejudiced beliefs. However, she loved to preach about her amazing values and prided herself on being a kind person. June did not care about others, and her kind persona was part of her fake social-media brand. She was vapid, self-centered, and obsessed with her appearance, and the people in her life were only around to serve her and cater to her narcissistic needs.

## Cameron: Danger Ahead

Cameron is a handsome, successful entrepreneur in his thirties who owns his own business. He is also a former professional athlete and an adrenaline junkie who loves to take risks. His Instagram page is full of photos of adventures in exotic places, or of him shirtless and working out. Almost every photo on his social media pages shows his perfectly sculpted body, which he spends many hours of the day maintaining. Although it is no secret to the outside observer that Cameron is incredibly self-absorbed and vain, there is a much darker story behind the seemingly harmless, albeit self-centered social media profile.

Cameron has been accused of multiple sexual assaults and uses his position of power as a successful business owner to intimidate women and make them feel uncomfortable. He has touched female employees inappropriately at work and sexually propositioned female employees of his. There have been several formal accusations against Cameron, but he is well-connected and has never faced any real ramifications, personally or professionally.

Commitment is not really Cameron's thing, and on the rare occasions he has been in a supposedly monogamous relationship, he has been a serial cheater and emotionally abusive. His relationships never last because, ultimately, Cameron has no real emotional investment in these women. He oscillates and is sometimes warm and affectionate, but most of the time he is cold and aloof. In the beginning of a relationship, he behaves like a typical narcissist. He pours on the charm and flattery but within a few months he begins to detach and become critical. He lacks empathy, and attachment to most people in his life and all of his relationships are shallow.

Perhaps the most confusing aspect of Cameron's personality is the fact that he is seemingly charitable and generous. He donates regularly to important causes and appears to be committed to social justice movements. He has traveled abroad on multiple humanitarian trips, and if you did not know him well, based on his social media persona, you might think he is the perfect catch: handsome, smart, philanthropic, and wealthy. If you attempt to get to know him well, you begin to see the cracks behind the perfectly filtered façade.

## THE NARCISSIST ON SOCIAL MEDIA: THE CHICKEN OR THE EGG?

Are June and Cameron narcissists? People often use the term *narcissist* casually, a buzzword of sorts, especially when describing how people present themselves on social media. This is natural since online platforms are the perfect breeding ground for vanity and self-obsession.

The word *narcissist* originated from the Greek myth of Narcissus. As the story goes, Narcissus was an incredibly handsome young man who one day happened to see his reflection in the water. He became so obsessed with himself, he eventually died of starvation because he could not tear himself away from his image. There are other versions of this story, but it is essentially a cautionary tale of self-obsession and vanity.

True clinical and pathological narcissism is much more complex than self-absorption and vanity. Chapter 1 will define what narcissism is and what it is not and the different subtypes of narcissism, and how they show up on social media. But first, let's explore the answers to these questions: Are social media and narcissism related? If so, why is their connection potentially harmful for society?

The studies that have been done on narcissism and social media have been interesting—and sometimes conflicting. Currently, billions of people around the world use social media networking sites (SNS) like Twitter, Instagram, Facebook, Snapchat, and TikTok, and people have been rightfully concerned about the influence and impact they are having on our psyches. Do narcissists gravitate toward social media more? Is social media making us more narcissistic? Scientists and researchers have attempted to shed more light on those questions with some compelling evidence to support the theory.

One major study showed narcissists are more likely to have a greater number of friends on social networking sites, and they also have a propensity to upload more photos and feel a strong connection to Facebook in particular.[1]

Another interesting study showed that problematic Internet use (PIU) predicted narcissism in those who primarily used visual social media.[2] PIU is defined as a digital dependency, or an addiction to Internet usage. Furthermore, there have been some interesting studies that suggest certain people have increasing narcissistic tendencies *after* social media use. One of these studies showed that people who were on the now-defunct, early personal sharing site MySpace for only fifteen minutes went on to score significantly higher on the narcissism scale.[3]

When thinking about problematic social media use as it relates to narcissism, it is crucial to note that the use of social media can be both positive and destructive. The feelings of validation that come from social media are incredibly addictive, but the invalidation that it can produce also feels really damaging to our sense of self-worth.

There is an important distinction to note between the motives of narcissists versus emotionally intelligent people in seeking out social media. It is normal for all human beings to want validation, appreciation, and to feel special, and wanting those things does not make someone a narcissist. However, social media is one of the easier ways to attain shallow and immediate gratification. It fills our deeply ingrained need for acceptance and validation, but only for a fleeting amount of time, and we soon want more. While narcissistic people tend to use social media specifically to gain admiration, attention, and followers, emotionally intelligent people use social media to connect with others and deepen relationships. The emotionally intelligent people who enjoy validation and appreciation are not using social media because they are looking for attention.

It is also important to look at how social media exacerbates narcissism within a given context. For example, in January of 2019, *Forbes* reported that 78 percent of Americans lived paycheck to paycheck.[4] Shockingly, this was more than a year before the COVID-19 pandemic plagued the world, causing even greater economic despair. In 2019, one in eight Americans were living below the poverty line.[5] These statistics are sobering. Many people struggle to make ends meet, and the cost of living continues to soar worldwide. Given all this, there is a vast disconnect between people who flaunt their wealth online and the average person who may be envious or crave the fairy-tale lifestyles that they are seeing on social media. Some may feel pressure to create this ultimately unattainable, "perfect" lifestyle.

The flaunting of wealth or material possessions, regardless of whether it is a real or false portrayal, is damaging to the viewer on social media. There are those who want the lifestyle they see others living. They note that companies in turn respond by asking the poster to contact them to promote their products, which then fuels the viewer's belief that this kind of accumulated wealth and the resultant lifestyle is easily attainable by becoming a social media influencer.

Even if people don't embark on "influencing" as a new career path, they can easily fall into the trap of comparing themselves with the posters of these fabulous lives that they don't have. They might create their own disingenuous posts about leading a life of material abundance, creating a vicious cycle of always wanting more and constantly struggling to keep up with the Joneses.

It is alluring to think that one could generate income simply by living your life and pressing a few buttons to upload photos and captions. Of course, the reality is much more work than that. To monetize your brand, you need to devote a significant amount of time to it—and to yourself. Spending much of the day focused on yourself and the image you portray to others—sometimes masses of complete strangers—is dangerously flirting with narcissism if you were not already narcissistic to begin with.

Furthermore, in our modern digital world, anyone who wants to own a business is told they need to have a "brand" and a "following" on social media. It continues to perpetuate a vicious cycle of feeling like your professional success is tied to an image or how many people follow you. The message we receive is that the more people who follow us, the more "important" we are.

The rise of social media and the addictive nature of "likes" and "follows" seems to be fueling a culture of narcissism. By putting a lot of energy and focus into a personal brand and convincing others to follow us, we can fall into a trap of becoming overly dedicated to our own self-importance.

The more we center on ourselves and obsess over the persona we are curating on our social media profiles, the more we lose our connection to other people. The more we worry about ourselves, the less we worry about others, and that erodes our empathy. Without empathy, it is impossible to have authentic relationships. Empathy, the ability to put ourselves in someone else's shoes, is what helps people feel cared for, supported, loved, and accepted. When people in any kind of relationship have mutual empathy, they nurture and respect each other, leading to mutual feelings of contentment and safety.

Anne Manne, a journalist, social philosopher, and author of an important book on the subject, *The Life of I: The New Culture of Narcissism,*[6] told me she believes that the relationship between social media users is an alchemy, a transformative process. She says our behavior can be influenced by seeing other people bragging, boasting, talking about their fabulous holidays, or showing off their perfect family because we are social creatures. It is inevitable that we will be impacted and influenced by what we see and observe in our social surroundings.

Manne also believes we need to look at the impact social media has on narcissism in a deeper way, saying:

It's not just extraordinarily trivial and self-involved and self-centered—it is. There is a book that looked at diaries of girls in the late nineteenth century and then looked at the diaries in the late twentieth century. The comparisons show that in the late nineteenth century, the girls were saying things like, *"I have to be nice. I have to be a better person."* Basically, the self is a moral project, and all of us know it's actually hard not to be selfish sometimes. It's hard to be good to people all the time when you're feeling crabby or tired, for example. These are effortful forms of attention to others, and it is not without cost to the individual. Fast forward to the twentieth century and all the diary entries were: *"I need to lose weight"* or *"I need to look better," "I need to get Botox or fillers in the lips," "I need to work on myself as a body project"* . . .

and this really took off with social media, so there's something hugely problematic about where the culture is headed.

W. Keith Campbell, social psychologist, professor, leading researcher on narcissism, and co-author of *The New Science of Narcissism: Understanding One of the Greatest Psychological Challenges of Our Time—and What You Can Do About It*,[7] shares a similar opinion, based on many years of research in the field of narcissism, telling me:

> Social media changes the social norms and the norms become: you've got to have white teeth, and a certain look, and if you don't have it you have to go for cosmetic treatment to get it. People are marketing body transformation because of body dysmorphia. A lot of this stuff is an issue.

It is important to emphasize that our intrinsic worth is never tied to how many people follow us or like our social media posts, how much money we make, or how many fancy material possessions we have collected. Many studies show that our happiness and worth is contingent upon how emotionally connected we are to others, which is the opposite of being self-focused. Focusing too much on ourselves, and things that do not ultimately matter, leads us to be more disconnected from others, less empathetic, more entitled, and eventually, miserable. Some of the unhappiest people seem to "have it all," both on and off social media. There are people who have shared that the more success, money, fame, adoration, and followers they acquired did not make them happier, and certainly did not increase their self-esteem.

Some of us believe that if we only had more money, respect, and/or success, we would be more fulfilled, but that just leads us further down a rabbit hole of narcissism, self-indulgence, and misery. Even so, with social media and the relatively new access to so many celebrities, influencers, and images of the "good life," many of us are constantly reminded of what we don't have and then think it's what we *should* have. Perhaps digital culture is leading us to want all the wrong things and is exacerbating an already toxic cycle of constant comparison. As Theodore Roosevelt aptly said, "Comparison is the thief of joy." And where do we do most of our comparison these days? On social media.

Of course, social media also has its benefits. For instance, modern technology and innovation have made life more transient and people move away from their families more, either for jobs or for a new adventure, and platforms like Facebook and Instagram give us the opportunity to stay connected to people from different chapters of our lives who might otherwise be hard to stay in touch with. There are also immense benefits when using social media to promote important humanitarian and social justice causes. Social media can be incredibly beneficial to entrepreneurs, and it can provide an innovative way for businesses to thrive and reach new customers.

In this book, I am not necessarily advocating a complete exodus from social media, nor am I telling anyone what they should definitively do with their social media accounts and their time. The use of social media can be a very personal thing, and I have come to believe that when it comes to our mental health, it is *how* we use it that is most important. We can let social media consume us, or we can use it in a modified and productive way. We can dictate how much we let it control us, or whether we need to shield ourselves from the narcissism we see playing out on social media, or maybe we just need to do some self-reflection on how social media may be influencing or bringing out narcissistic behavior in us.

Some of the concerns I have about social media are that the intoxicating and addicting aspects of it can potentially make us more narcissistic, but in more cases, it is most likely revealing who the narcissistic people in our lives are. To me, the most fascinating aspect of social media is that we can stay connected to people we normally would not have before, and then we see aspects of their personalities that we would not necessarily have seen if we had just interacted with them in real life. Seeing people's personality traits and unfiltered opinions online often colors how we see them and our relationships with them, sometimes for the worse.

There is something about being behind a keyboard with a lack of face-to-face interaction that emboldens people to say things they would not otherwise say if you were with them in person. Witnessing people's unfiltered thoughts can be a good way to find out who someone really is, but it can also be exhausting when we are constantly bombarded by other people's thoughts and opinions—especially if we aren't close to them. Sometimes, we like people better when we only know them in passing—at work or in our communities. Social media might reveal an entirely different aspect to them that changes how we feel about them, minus the ability to really understand their perspective.

Another way in which social media is fueling our narcissistic tendencies is the fact that it is mindless and easy to constantly post photos of the minutiae of your life. Those closest to us may want to know the tiny details of our lives, but have we come to a point where we share, and even boast about, how great our jobs, partners, and lives are to hundreds (and sometimes thousands) of people we don't really know well, if at all?

Do we even want lots of people who are not truly invested in our lives and our well-being to know intimate and personal things about us? To see photos of our children? To know how many times we worked out that week? And why do we want to do this? What are we trying to prove? Are we simply just sharing our joy, or is there something else going on?

The answers to these questions are complex and will be explored more thoroughly in this book. But before we begin to examine how social media might make us more narcissistic and how social media can easily exacerbate existing narcissism in people who are already narcissistic, we must understand what narcissism is, what it is not, and the different ways it can manifest. Not all narcissism is alike, and there are varying degrees of narcissism, all on a spectrum. Learning to recognize when the people in our lives are too narcissistic to reform is helpful, and one of the ways we can recognize these types of dangerous narcissists is seeing how they present themselves online.

How can we recognize when social media is making us more narcissistic and less connected from humanity? How do we protect our children from the allure of social media that tends to encourage narcissism? My hope is that by exploring these questions, we can look more deeply at how social media has the potential to make us and the people around us more narcissistic, but on the flip side, how we can learn to use social media to encourage qualities and traits that are the opposite of narcissism: fostering empathy, connection with others, and a sense of community.

# Chapter 1

# NARCISSISM DEFINED: SELFIE CULTURE OR SOMETHING MORE?

We need look no further than the photo on the cover of this book to see selfie culture in action. Undoubtedly, you've seen people posing in front of their phones—at the museum, at the park, in front of landmarks—completely oblivious to everything and everyone around them. You might think to yourself, *What a narcissist!* But is that really the case? Self-centered and oblivious, for certain, but is this *really* narcissism?

*Narcissist* and *narcissism* get bandied about in casual conversations and appear in headlines more than ever because of the popularity of social media. However, the true definition of a narcissist can be far more threatening to society than someone who merely blocks traffic on a stairwell to get that perfect shot for Instagram.

## THE WIDE SPECTRUM OF NARCISSISM

So, what does it mean to be a true narcissist, at least in the clinical sense? Before we can dissect the traits of a clinical narcissist, it is important to understand that many of the top experts and researchers in the field believe that narcissism—like most personality traits—exists on a spectrum. This means that we all have some narcissism in us, and this is not necessarily a bad thing. There are some positive aspects to narcissism, and in fact, moderate narcissism is considered to be healthy.

Dr. Craig Malkin, a psychologist and author of *Rethinking Narcissism,*[8] argues that moderate narcissism is what allows us to believe in ourselves, take risks, and do things in life with the belief we can succeed. Healthy narcissism is recognizing and considering the needs of other people while simultaneously having good boundaries and honoring your own needs.

Dr. Malkin discusses narcissism on a spectrum between zero to ten, with people who are the most dangerously narcissistic falling somewhere between an eight and ten on the scale. Those who are in the middle of the scale and have a healthy sense of self will be somewhere around a five. People who may have little self-worth fall extremely low on the scale, around a zero to two.

When we look at extreme narcissism, around the eight to ten on the spectrum, Dr. Malkin uses a term he calls "Triple E" to define when narcissism becomes pathological and dangerous. Triple E stands for Empathy Impairments, Entitlement, and Exploitation. A person with pathological narcissism will possess all these things to varying degrees. At its worst, Triple E will result in things like pathological lying, extortion, bribery, fraud, theft, money laundering, violence, all types of abuse, kidnapping, murder, racism, and war.

There are times in life where even well-meaning and overall "good" people will have empathy impairments, exploit others, and act entitled. It is impossible for a human to have empathy all the time. For example, an interesting research study in 2013 led by Tania Singer from the Max Planck Institute for Human Cognitive and Brain Sciences found that "Our own feelings can distort our capacity for empathy . . . or when we have to make particularly quick decisions, our empathy is severely limited."[9]

In addition to the brain not always being equipped for instantaneous empathy, humans become defensive when they feel threatened, and that reduces our capacity for empathy. In Imago Relationship Theory (a form of relationship and couples therapy that focuses on transforming conflict into healing and growth through relational connection), in which I am certified, we learn that people become defensive when they feel unsafe in their relationships (this is not just about feeling physically unsafe, but emotionally unsafe).

Whenever we feel unsafe, we react in some way. This usually leads us to have several responses, including but not limited to, shouting, aggression, shutting down, defensiveness, stonewalling (a refusal to communicate), and criticizing. We cannot connect with others in a meaningful way when we are in that state of mind, and it is really hard to empathize with another person in that moment—even with those we love most. When human beings are in survival mode because of a perceived threat, the brain has a reduced capacity for empathy. It is operating from a very primitive part, not accessed by logic, so even if the threat is not dangerous in actuality, we respond with behaviors that can be destructive to our relationships. It is like killing a mosquito with a flame thrower.

Entitlement is something I see often in generally well-meaning people who would not be considered narcissists by the clinical definition. Entitlement, the inherent belief that you deserve special treatment or privileges over others, is an obnoxious way to behave at best. Entitled people also believe they can break certain rules or societal norms that are put in place to benefit the community, even when others are following those guidelines. For instance, think of the person who waits for someone in the "fire lane, no parking" area outside the grocery store even when there are ample spaces in the parking lot. Even though there is no fire truck in sight, if everyone did this, there would be a big problem if there was an emergency.

When explaining entitlement to my young children, I use the example of what it means to be a good guest in someone's home. If you go to someone's home and they ask you to take your shoes off when you enter, you take your shoes off. You may think that rule is silly, or you may not have that rule in your house, but it doesn't matter. You abide by the rules whenever you are on someone else's property or place of business. We saw a lot of this type of entitlement during the COVID-19 pandemic when people would knowingly violate the rules that a business had in place.

Entitlement is also about feeling and acting superior to others. People in positions of power sometimes feel entitled to special treatment and might abuse their power to get special favors or access to things that others would not be able to. Conversely, people without much power can also act entitled in their social circles and communities because it is a way for them to feel superior, powerful, and in control. Those who are insecure at their core need to feel superior and in control. They act entitled to cover up for their insecurities, or they are narcissists who believe they are entitled to whatever they want at the expense of other people. Some people would argue that it's both—that narcissists are insecure and entitled.

As for exploitation, the *Cambridge Dictionary* definition is: "The use of something in order to get an advantage from it," as well as, "The act of using someone unfairly for your own advantage."[10] Exploitation is a main feature of a narcissistic personality, but again, even people who are not narcissistic and do not qualify for the personality disorder may exploit others from time to time. For instance, a boss might make someone work overtime without extra pay, with the justification that it is needed to complete a job. It is important to understand that true narcissists exploit others on a relatively regular basis. It is a pervasive pattern that is a consistent feature of their personality.

Human beings are not perfect, nor will we ever be. It is unrealistic to think that we can be nice, kind, empathetic, and generous all the time. There are also perfectly good reasons why we should not be when we live in a world where people can take advantage of our kindness. Having firm boundaries is just as important as being kind. Unfortunately, some are conditioned to believe that having boundaries and saying "no" without an explanation is callous. It is important to know that protecting yourself, being firm with others, and delineating boundaries is neither unkind nor selfish. It is vitally important to our emotional well-being. Still, many of us have difficulty establishing boundaries because we have been taught to be people pleasers and feel guilty when we don't automatically do what others expect of us. But this is dangerous; squelching our own needs and desires can later manifest as resentment, anxiety, and depression.

# NARCISSISTIC SUPPLY, NARCISSISTIC RAGE, AND FLYING MONKEYS

Understanding how narcissists operate on social media and in everyday life requires knowing what they thrive on how they respond to situations, and how they use other people around them to get to and hurt their targets.

## Supply

Narcissistic supply is one of the most important pieces of knowledge one can have when trying to understand narcissism and identifying a narcissist. *Narcissistic supply is what all narcissists need and will do anything to get.* Narcissistic supply is attention, adoration, admiration, and anything that makes a narcissist feel uniquely special and superior.

As we will soon explore, there are different means that a narcissist uses to get supply, both agentic and communal. *Agentic* means are usually obvious and self-serving ways to get supply. On social media, this might be posting highly filtered selfies, obvious and arrogant self-promotion, and relentless bragging.

"Communal" means to appear altruistic on the surface. In this case, someone might post about all the good deeds they have done or anything that makes them look favorable in relation to their community.

In either case, supply is oxygen to narcissists. They feel empty without it, and they are addicted to getting it. Social media is a fertile ground for supply to narcissists, which can be both agentic, communal, or a combination on the various platforms. However, when the narcissist doesn't acquire supply, they can become spiteful and angry.

For a dangerous narcissist on the high end of the spectrum of narcissism, other people—even children—are just objects who fill them with supply; that is their only use for the people in their lives. The narcissist only keeps others around them if they serve a purpose—which is to give the narcissist attention and admiration. Once the narcissist finds no use for someone, they will discard them and leave them behind as if they never existed. A dangerous narcissist has no real attachments to anyone. Any interest they show in another person is simply an act. They love to lay on the charm in the beginning because they know this show of generosity and adoration is the perfect way to get you hooked on them. Once the narcissist takes off their mask and reveals their true self, they are incredibly cruel and often abusive, emotionally or otherwise.

## Rage

Narcissistic rage is the narcissist's response to any perceived threat, rejection, or insult. Their anger can be explosive, or it can be passive-aggressive, which often manifests as acting cold, rejecting, or withdrawn. In either case, the anger is usually extreme, even if it is the more internalized type and not belligerent or loud. Where social media is concerned, narcissistic rage can potentially be triggered by things such as a post not getting enough attention or likes, and the reaction is to lash out with aggressive behavior or cyberbullying. Anything on social media that could cause a narcissist to feel rejected, threatened, or criticized (and there are many ways social media aggravates those negative feelings for anyone who uses it regularly) can spark not only rage, but even worse, retaliation. When a narcissist decides to retaliate against a real or perceived slight on social media, things can get very ugly.

## Flying Monkeys

The term "flying monkeys" comes from the movie *The Wizard of Oz*. The Wicked Witch of the West sends winged monkeys to capture

Dorothy and her dog Toto and bring them to her. The monkeys have an unwavering loyalty to the witch, even if that loyalty means hurting themselves in the process. The scene is disturbingly creepy, and the monkeys terrorize not only Dorothy and Toto, but her friends: the Tin Man, the Cowardly Lion, and the Scarecrow.

The same concept of the Wicked Witch of the West and her furry henchmen applies to the narcissist. "Flying monkeys" is a pop psychology term to describe the people the narcissist uses to do their dirty work. You can find this unholy alliance everywhere—in families, among friends, at work, and in politics. Once the narcissist has identified a target, they will use the flying monkeys to gossip, spread rumors, relay messages, and torment the victim. The monkeys are easily manipulated by the narcissist and will believe the lies without question. Sometimes, flying monkeys are also narcissists.

On social media, flying monkeys can do all sorts of damage. A clear example would be cyberbullying. People can spread vicious rumors, send threatening messages, and make mean and nasty comments about people's photos and on their pages. Flying monkeys can be used by the narcissist to spy on their target, particularly monitoring their activity on social media. These types of aggressions on social media can have very dire consequences. In certain cases, severe cyberbullying (especially by groups of bullies) has turned deadly, sometimes ending in suicide or self-harm.

## SELF-ABSORPTION AND NARCISSISM— ARE THEY THE SAME THING?

Before I delve into the different types of narcissists and how they present themselves on social media, it is important to define what true narcissism *isn't*. We are now living in a world teeming with so-called "reality" television and social media. Anyone, if they try, can be a celebrity or a social media influencer with the potential to amass a large following. Prior to the digital age, it would have been nearly impossible for someone who was not a talented musician, athlete, or actor to achieve the kind of fame that we see now. Today, talentless people become overnight sensations for engaging in ridiculous and sometimes downright dangerous things—famous for being famous.

The world certainly seems more narcissistic than ever before if our definition of narcissism is only about self-absorption, fame-seeking, and looking for unhealthy amounts of attention. The important distinction to make here is that although narcissists are all self-absorbed and crave attention (either overtly or even secretly), true narcissists must also have little to no empathy for others and also engage in actions that hurt other people and cause lasting damage.

Self-absorption is defined by *Merriam-Webster's Dictionary* as "absorbed in one's own thoughts, activities, or interests."[11] While all self-absorbed people are consumed with themselves, it does not mean they are necessarily lacking in empathy. It is entirely possible that a person who is very self-focused can still have empathy for others. Vanity does not equal cruelty. The vain and self-absorbed are excessively preoccupied with their own appearance and achievements and live in their own world where they are the main focus.

Self-absorption is not a good thing, nor something for which we should strive. People who are self-absorbed generally have difficulty with close relationships because they are so focused on their own experience that they don't understand important social cues. An example of this would be when you are going through a hard time and a friend talks excessively about their problems, seemingly oblivious to your pain. While sometimes people are uncomfortable and don't know how to handle a difficult conversation, there are others who act this way intentionally, and they are most likely higher on the spectrum of narcissism. A self-absorbed person who is not a true narcissist does not have this same intention. Unfortunately, some people are so self-involved, they are not thinking about your perspective and how they can best support you, but it does not mean they act with malice. It is more a lack of self-awareness than anything else.

It is also important to mention that some people who may appear self-absorbed on the surface are actually suffering from depression, anxiety, PTSD (post-traumatic stress disorder), or complex PTSD (CPTSD). These things can be very debilitating and beyond someone's control. It is critical to be aware, compassionate, and sensitive to these conditions. As the psychologist Dr. Leon F. Seltzer correctly says, "Individuals with an anxiety disorder are 'afflicted' with self-absorption not because they are selfish or insensitive to others (as are narcissists), but because they are locked into bothersome, repetitive thought processes reflecting fears both about their personal adequacy and how others might (adversely) see them."[12]

PTSD, CPTSD, and trauma can cause people to feel fearful, anxious, and unsafe, among many other things. Living with this ominous cloud overhead will make someone hypervigilant and can hinder the person from thinking outside of themselves because they are trying to survive in a world that feels terrifying and threatening. Furthermore, people who are clinically depressed have a hard time finding motivation; even getting out of bed to face the day can be an insurmountable challenge. They are sad, fatigued, and exhausted and do not have the energy to engage with the world. This may seem like self-absorption, but it is not.

Because a person who may seem like a narcissist on social media may be suffering from something like depression, anxiety, or PTSD, it is so important to define narcissism in a truly clear and accurate way. Someone may be self-absorbed, but they are not a narcissist as defined by Craig Malkin's Triple E, in addition to the criteria for the different subtypes of narcissism, which we will soon explore.

## A TRAUMA-INFORMED APPROACH TO NARCISSISM

Trauma and narcissism often go together. It is essential to take a trauma-informed approach and to understand that being parented by, in a relationship with, or even being subjected regularly to a narcissistic person can result in a trauma response. The life-altering consequences can be debilitating and prevent people from trusting others.

According to the *Harvard Medical School Health Blog*,[13] "The CDC statistics on abuse and violence in the United States are sobering. They report that one in four children experiences some sort of maltreatment (physical, sexual, or emotional abuse). One in four women has experienced domestic violence. In addition, one in five women and one in seventy-one men have experienced rape at some point in their lives—12 percent of these women and 30 percent of these men were younger than ten years old when they were raped. This means a very large number of people have experienced serious trauma at some point in their lives."

*The Substance Abuse and Mental Health Service's Administration's (SAMHSA) Concept of Trauma and Guidance for a Trauma-Informed Approach* says: "Individual trauma results from an event, series of events, or set of circumstances that is experienced by an individual as physically or emotionally harmful or life-threatening and that has lasting adverse effects on the individual's functioning and mental, physical, social, emotional, or spiritual well-being."[14]

A trauma-informed approach requires the understanding that trauma is present in many forms. A traumatic experience changes how you fundamentally see the world, impacting your feelings of trust and safety. Many of us understand trauma to come from violence, war, rape, and other incredibly frightening circumstances. Other types of traumas can arise from surviving a life-threatening illness, years of emotional abuse, witnessing a traumatic event as a bystander, bullying, and many other things.

A trauma-informed approach to mental health is critical because it brings awareness and compassion to how people respond to traumatic events and stress. It also gives trauma survivors the opportunity to receive the appropriate help they need to heal, which should, in most cases, be done with professionals specifically trained in evidence-based trauma treatments.

Many people abuse substances to cope with trauma. Addressing the root trauma that may have led to the substance-abuse problem in the first place is essential. Survivors of narcissistic abuse are also traumatized to varying degrees. Helping these survivors name what they are experiencing is incredibly important in their healing process.

Someone who has had past or ongoing trauma may be confused with having narcissistic traits or behaviors, because some people who seek incessant attention as adults have experienced developmental trauma as children. Best said by Dr. Bill Gordon in his article, "Excessive Attention-Seeking and Drama Addiction":

> Excessive attention-seeking is not a character flaw. It is a brain wiring response to early developmental trauma caused by neglect. The developing brain observes its environment and wires itself accordingly to survive in that world that it presumes will be like those experiences.[15]

There is also research that some personality disorders may also arise from childhood neglect. According to Dr. David P. Bernstein, "Many patients with personality disorders report that emotional maltreatment by family members was a central and painful aspect of their upbringing."

Dr. Bill Gordon also says that childhood neglect results in the wiring of the brain to associate a lack of attention with danger. He explains how addiction to drama can relate to the wiring of our brains:

> The obvious answer is drama gets attention. However, it is more than that. Drama causes the pituitary gland and hypothalamus to secrete endorphins, which are the pain-suppressing and pleasure-inducing compounds, which heroin and other *opiates* mimic. Hence, drama eases the anxiety of wanting more attention than you are getting. Naturally, since drama uses the same mechanisms in the brain as opiates, people can easily become addicted to drama.

Therefore, there can be a significant difference between a disordered narcissist and a person who pursues too much attention and validation due to a traumatic upbringing. A narcissist may also have endured developmental trauma, but the relentless need and addiction to attention doesn't equate to a lack of empathy, entitlement, or exploitation. Rather, it may be the brain's response to developmental trauma.

## THE SUBTYPES OF NARCISSISM AND HOW THEY PRESENT ON SOCIAL MEDIA

Below, we'll examine the various subtypes of narcissism: malignant narcissism, vulnerable or covert narcissism, communal narcissism, and collective narcissism.

## Narcissistic Personality Disorder and Malignant Narcissism

When I was in graduate school, the first class I took was called Psychopathology. Psychopathology, the study of mental disorders, partly focuses on the category that mental health professionals refer to as "personality disorders." Personality disorders differ from mood disorders (depression, anxiety, schizophrenia, post-traumatic stress disorder, etc.) because they are patterns of behavior that cause problems, especially in relationships. Mood disorders are thought to have a biological cause. Of course, mood disorders and personality disorders can both be present in an individual, and it can also be difficult to distinguish between them.

As a young graduate student, I learned that the personality disorders in the *Diagnostic and Statistical Manual of Mental Disorders* (the DSM) were considered to be rare and only diagnosable when strict criteria were met. Narcissistic personality disorder (NPD) in the DSM is the personality disorder most people are familiar with, and it is only thought to be present in 1 percent of the population. However, different studies do show some variations in the prevalence of NPD. In order to meet the criteria to be considered for a diagnosis of NPD, the individual must have: "A pervasive pattern of grandiosity (in fantasy or behavior), a constant need for admiration, and a lack of empathy, beginning by early adulthood and present in a variety of contexts, as indicated by the presence of at least five of the following nine criteria:

- A grandiose sense of self-importance
- A preoccupation with fantasies of unlimited success, power, brilliance, beauty, or ideal love
- A belief that he or she is special and unique and can only be understood by, or should associate with, other special or high-status people or institutions

- A need for excessive admiration
- A sense of entitlement
- Interpersonally exploitive behavior
- A lack of empathy
- Envy of others or a belief that others are envious of him or her
- A demonstration of arrogant and haughty behaviors or attitudes

In a proposed alternative model cited in DSM-5, NPD is characterized by moderate or greater impairment in personality functioning, manifested by characteristic difficulties in two or more of the following four areas [2]:

- Identity
- Self-direction
- Empathy
- Intimacy"[16]

This description of a narcissist is accurate but does not encompass all the different ways in which narcissism presents. NPD can be relatively easy to spot because the classic narcissist is quite obviously grandiose and attention seeking.

The clinical definition of NPD also does not elaborate on the fact that a narcissistic person can be charming and appear to have empathy, which is part of the reason narcissistic people can be so dangerous. Their ability to masquerade as an empathetic and kind person is eerily precise. Dangerously narcissistic people can appear to be the kindest person in the room, and they can wear this disguise for a long time before you see their true colors.

## What Does NPD Look Like on Social Media?

Of course, we cannot label someone as a narcissist solely based on their social media profile. However, there may be some clues to how someone with NPD might present themselves on social media. The most obvious sign of a narcissist and how they present themselves on social media is when they post or use certain words and language that could draw attention to themselves. Some of this language could be aggressive or sexual in nature.[17]

While selfie posting also seems to be correlated with narcissism, one study has shown that selfie posting has a stronger link with male narcissists.[18] Selfie posting can be done alone, with a partner, or in group selfies.

However, there have been other cross-cultural studies in which selfie posting is also a characteristic of narcissistic women. In one study,[19] participants were from three different geographic communities and the women in this study posted more selfies than men. These women were more likely to be histrionic (overly theatrical and melodramatic in character and style) and grandiose. Another study revealed that narcissists were more likely to wear flashy, expensive clothes and spend a great deal of time on their appearance (women wearing lots of makeup and showing cleavage were part of this presentation).[20]

Because the typical grandiose narcissist thrives off of constant attention, social media is an attractive way for them to easily get it. A person high on the spectrum of narcissism may very well be obvious on social media. They may wear flashy clothing, post a lot of selfies, use aggressive or attention-seeking language, and post constantly. They may also boast regularly and post things that are designed to elicit jealousy from others. Not only is this a way to seek attention, but they also enjoy making others upset.

All these aspects of how someone presents themselves on social media can certainly give us insight into someone's potential narcissistic traits. A narcissist may also use social media to intimidate and abuse, which is indicative of their inherent cruelty. Stalking and trolling are just a few ways a narcissist will use social media to inflict damage and pain on others, and this will be further explored in a later chapter.

Cameron, the handsome entrepreneur from the Introduction, is an example of what NPD looks like on social media. His incessant posting without his shirt in various poses and his large following in the tens of thousands indicates that he could be a narcissist. Behind the social media facade, we see that his exploitation of others at work, lack of attachment to anyone, and the incidents where he was the perpetrator of multiple sexual assaults (that he was able to get away with) further confirm that he is a narcissist who inflicts harm upon others without remorse.

## The Vulnerable Narcissist (aka the Covert Narcissist)

Vulnerable narcissism, also known as covert narcissism, can look quite different from overt and grandiose narcissism. The desire for attention and the need to feel superior is the common theme with *all* narcissists, but the vulnerable narcissist may appear quiet, self-deprecating, humble, and even introverted. They may also act self-conscious, whereas a grandiose narcissist will exhibit confidence and charm.

Although vulnerable narcissists seem quiet and unassuming, they believe they are uniquely special even if they don't project that thought to the world at large. The disconnect between how others see them versus how they see themselves makes them angry inside. All narcissists are thin-skinned, but vulnerable narcissists are hypersensitive to criticism. Many of them harbor fantasies of recognition for their greatness and often daydream about fame. They feel a tremendous amount of self-pity because the world does not see them as influential and notable.

Vulnerable narcissists are high on the scale of neuroticism. In the field of psychology, neuroticism means that a person tends to skew more toward anxious, depressive, and self-doubting and possesses a general negativity. Those who are higher on the neuroticism scale tend to worry a lot, are irritable, moody, full of self-doubt, lacking in resilience, feel that minor problems are too much to handle, and have high levels of negativity.

Dr. Berit Brogaard, a philosopher specializing in cognitive neuroscience, describes the main difference between grandiose and vulnerable narcissism as such:

> Grandiose narcissism is characterized by extraversion, low neuroticism and overt expressions of feelings of superiority and entitlement, whereas covert narcissism is marked by introspective self-absorbedness, high neuroticism, and alternating feelings of excessive pride and deep shame.[21]

To the outside world, the vulnerable/covert narcissist may seem like your average nice person. Behind closed doors, they can inflict pain and hostility toward those closest to them.

## What Does Vulnerable/Covert Narcissism Look Like on Social Media?

Vulnerable narcissism is tricky to spot, especially if you do not know the person well. Often, vulnerable narcissists are only seen for who they *really* are by those closest to them (their spouse or romantic partner and immediate family members). Their friends, neighbors, and community may have no clue that behind closed doors they are emotionally abusive and cruel. If the vulnerable narcissist is hard to discern in real life interactions, they may be even harder to spot on social media because the general understanding by the public is that a narcissist is loud and flashy.

A vulnerable narcissist will not necessarily outwardly boast, take selfies, or post things that are attention seeking, but they may still use social media to serve their purposes of gaining narcissistic supply. A scorned vulnerable narcissist may stalk you, bully you, or post things to intentionally upset you. For example, passive-aggressively posting a photo from a gathering to which you were not invited but otherwise would not have known about: "Best party ever! Thanks again for the invite. Whoever missed this, missed out!"

## Andrea: The Million-Dollar Imposter

Those who first meet Andrea describe her as sweet, charming, and humble. They'd be surprised that she's always dreamed of being famous and that someday, she would be important, special, and recognized by everyone in her field. She is thirty-five and a brilliant virologist and studied at several prestigious schools.

Those closest to Andrea know a different side of her. Lacking in empathy, she has a hard time seeing other people's perspectives, especially if they get in the way of her desires. Andrea hires help but treats them poorly, believing they should be grateful to have a job. Several former employees of Andrea's left because they couldn't deal with her superiority complex and her cruelty.

While she'd never admit it, and although she goes to great lengths for it to appear otherwise, she even puts her own needs before her children's and her husband's. In reality, she expects adoration and attention from her family, but she hardly reciprocates. She does just enough for them so she will look good to the outside world. Andrea is the type of narcissist who does everything for the sake of appearances, so everything she does for her children is so she can appear to be an amazing mother. The thing about narcissistic mothers is that young children are only deserving of praise or affection if they fit the exact template of what the narcissistic mother wants. As long as Andrea's children go along with whatever she wants and have no opinions of their own, she will dote on them. However, if they deviate from her idealized version of them, she will withdraw and become cold and punitive. Her perfectly crafted social media image features photos of her million-dollar-plus suburban home, professional pictures of her beautiful children and handsome husband who look like they stepped out of a J. Crew catalog, and her professionally groomed purebred dog. Andrea doesn't particularly like people and is only interested in them when she can somehow benefit. She expects everyone around her to drop everything for her. How does she get them to comply? After years of practice, she knows how to turn on the flattery, with a syrupy sweet voice and a list of disingenuous compliments designed to butter up her targets to do her bidding.

Although Andrea believes she should be recognized for how amazing she is, there is another part of her that is deeply self-loathing. Andrea suffers from imposter syndrome, as do many who are not narcissists. Many narcissists like Andrea live with a gnawing fear that deep down, they will be discovered as frauds. Andrea dreads that someone will figure out she is not as smart or notable as she would like them to think she is. That aspect of herself is part of what drives her cruelty. When she feels bad about herself, she lashes out at others with narcissistic rage. The tirades are relentless. They can be tantrums of crying and yelling that last for days, and long written diatribes on text message, victimizing herself while criticizing whomever she is lashing out at. When one of her nannies quit unexpectedly because they could no longer take her abuse, she found out who their new employer was and sent them and the nanny text messages about how they would be sorry.

Because she feels powerless, she likes to exert control and will sometimes try to wield power over others by gaslighting them (saying things that make the other person question their sanity or judgment), throwing tantrums until she gets her way, and always trying to get the upper hand in any situation.

When Andrea was finally asked to do television interviews on her professional area of expertise, she was elated. Finally, she thought, others would recognize her as the go-to expert in her field, an important scholar with a brilliant mind. Although Andrea is cruel, selfish, and manipulative and fits the criteria for narcissism, she does not appear to be a grandiose narcissist on social media. She does not post excessively (although she does post with the objective of getting likes and admiration), she does not take selfies, and she dresses conservatively.

However, tiny glimpses of her narcissistic tendencies on social media come through when you start paying attention. She is obsessed with seeing herself on television, and she loves to take photographs of herself on screen. Recently, she has been using the photos of her televised interviews on her social media profiles. It is a way of showing other people how important she is.

Andrea uses social media for narcissistic supply, but she is savvy enough to understand that grandiosity can be off-putting to others, and part of her false persona is portraying herself as humble and sweet. Andrea wants to be liked and admired by everyone and knows that boasting and selfies are not the best way to get others to admire her.

It's perfectly normal to want to share our accomplishments and our lives with our friends and family—there is nothing narcissistic about that. The difference between Andrea and the average person is that she uses social media solely for admiration and validation. Taking photos of her television interviews and using them for her profiles also does not mean she is a narcissist on its own, but taking that information, along with her penchant for exploiting others, her entitlement, and her lack of empathy gives us clues into what sort of person she is at her core—a vulnerable narcissist who lashes out at others for not recognizing her importance, catering to her every need, and filling her with a narcissistic supply of attention and admiration.

## Communal Narcissism

Communal narcissism, a relatively new type of narcissism, has recently garnered more attention in the past ten years. An important study in 2012[22] made a distinction between agentic narcissism (self-serving) and communal narcissism (involved in community and helping others). The motives for both agentic and communal narcissists are the same; however, they differ in the means they use to acquire narcissistic supply. Communal narcissists pride themselves on being helpful, trustworthy, charitable, kind, and generous. Agentic narcissists are the classic grandiose narcissist. They do not feel a need to be seen as helpful or trustworthy, and they use selfish means to get what they want: attention, admiration, and power.

The communal narcissist also wants admiration, attention, and on many occasions, power, but they know they can get narcissistic supply by *acting* like a good and virtuous person. On the surface, communal narcissists can seem very agreeable, helpful, and positive, whereas the agentic/grandiose narcissist can be aggressive, dominating, and ruthless.

The intentions behind the communal narcissist's good deeds are not the desire to genuinely help others, but rather the need to feel important and special. By being the most helpful and trustworthy person in the room, they inflate their self-esteem and think they are morally superior and uniquely special. They believe their good deeds and communal work separate them from the rest, and they want to believe they are superior to those who surround them.

You often find the communal narcissist volunteering their time and energy to worthy causes. They can be religious leaders, PTA presidents, directors of non-profits, journalists, in helping professions (such as, doctors, nurses, or therapists), or self-proclaimed philanthropists who host fancy galas and frequently donate their money to charity. They do not necessarily have to be in positions of power, although the more grandiose they are, the more they believe they have the power to "save" or "change" the world through their good deeds.

The Communal Narcissism Inventory (CNI)[23] was developed to assess the communal narcissist. The CNI assessment looks for grandiose self-thoughts in the communal domain, as opposed to the agentic domain. In other words, "communal narcissism reflects high self-perceived capacity in communal domains, such as morality, kindness, and emotional intimacy."[24] The questions on the inventory range are as follows, and those taking the inventory mark their agreement on a scale of 1 to 7 (1 equaling do not agree, to 7, strongly agree):

- I am the most helpful person I know
- I am going to bring peace and justice to the world
- I am the best friend someone can have
- I will be well known for the good deeds I will have done
- I am (going to be) the best parent on this planet
- I am the most caring person in my social surroundings
- In the future, I will be well known for solving the world's problems
- I greatly enrich others' lives
- I will bring freedom to the people
- I am an amazing listener
- I will be able to solve world poverty
- I have a very positive influence on others
- I am generally the most understanding person
- I'll make the world a much more beautiful place
- I am extraordinarily trustworthy
- I will be famous for increasing people's well-being.

The more someone strongly agrees with these statements, the higher they will be on the CNI.

From this inventory, some of these self-thoughts seem very grandiose, such as, "I will be famous for increasing people's well-being," "I will bring freedom to the people," and "I will be able to solve world poverty," but more of these self-thoughts have to do with how a person impacts the people in their immediate circles or in their smaller communities. A communal narcissist can be someone who desires to gain power and admiration for changing the world on a larger level, but they may also feed off the attention of family and friends and enjoy simply being a big fish in a small pond.

J. E. Gebauer and his colleagues at Humboldt University in Berlin found a positive correlation between a concept called unmitigated communion and communal narcissism: Unmitigated communion is defined as "a focus on and involvement with others to the exclusion of the self."[25] Is unmitigated communion identical to communal narcissism? Do communal narcissists do things for others at the expense of themselves? Communal narcissists will surely do things at the expense of themselves and will pride themselves on being a martyr who sacrifices for others. Often, if they are not outwardly praised, they will make sure you know how self-sacrificing they are. This is another way that they feel morally superior to others. The communal narcissist may not act as entitled and exploitative as an agentic/grandiose narcissist, but this is only because acting entitled and exploiting others goes against the communal persona they have created to present to the world.

Gebauer and his colleagues also found a positive correlation between communal narcissists, communal orientation, and exchange orientation: Individuals who operate with communal orientation are concerned with the needs of others and want to help because they have other people's best interest at heart. In contrast, individuals high on exchange orientation operate in relationships where it is more tit for tat—*I do something for you with the expectation that I will get something in return,* not *because it simply benefits you and is a nice thing to do.* With communal orientation, there is not necessarily an expectation that one will get something in return for their good deed or thoughtful gesture. However, those with the trait of communal orientation may expect that other people automatically operate in the world in the same way that they do. The expectation that other people will operate the same way as we would under any given circumstance can get us into trouble because people do not have the same reactions to events. People get disappointed when others do not have the same reactions or behave in the ways they do, especially when it comes to morals and values.

Ultimately, the communal narcissist gets what they need by acting in a caring and thoughtful way. They also expect that they should get something in *return,* whether that is from a return of a favor, in praise, validation, or admiration. It is important to note that there is still plenty we do not know about communal narcissism. It's a relatively new concept, and I am sure that as more studies are conducted, we will see a wide range of behaviors and presentations of the communal narcissist.

## What Does Communal Narcissism Look Like on Social Media?

On social media, communal narcissism is easier to spot than vulnerable narcissism, especially when we know what to look for. Once people know what communal narcissism is, almost everyone can think of someone they know who they suspect is one. I have spoken to people who believe they have communal narcissists in their family, and even others who realize they have been married to a communal narcissist. These communal narcissists have sometimes been regarded as pillars of the community and are often engaged in numerous philanthropic and charitable initiatives.

On the darker side of the spectrum, I have heard of missionaries doing self-sacrificing and communal work, yet behind the scenes engaging in nefarious behaviors, sometimes as reprehensible and unforgiving as child abuse. These are more extreme versions of the communal narcissist, and of course there are some who are not at all in the public eye but still act trustworthy, caring, and selfless as a way of gaining narcissistic supply. For communal narcissists, there is no easier way to gain narcissistic supply than from an audience on social media, always at the fingertips.

Grandiose narcissists are perceived more unfavorably than communal narcissists on social media. One study looked at how people perceived agentic versus communal narcissistic status updates on Facebook.[26] The study revealed that agentic narcissist statuses were viewed more harshly than the others. This makes sense because grandiose and arrogant behavior, online and elsewhere, is generally off-putting to most people. Gestures and acts of goodwill, however, are seen as community-minded and are rewarded—seen as altruistic rather than self-serving. Some might argue, does the intent really matter if good is being done for others? If the communal narcissist is not harming anyone, then maybe it does not matter as much. As with all dangerous narcissism, a firm line needs to be drawn if the communal narcissist is engaging in behaviors that hurt or exploit others. Like all narcissism, communal narcissism[27] can exist on a spectrum with some communal narcissists being relatively harmless and others being quite dangerous.

Ultimately, understanding the communal narcissist on social media is knowing that what they do in public is to advance their image, and what they do in private may completely contradict their outward persona. A study on communal narcissism showed that communal narcissists who are publicly pro-environmental use that as way for them to feel special or superior. They may publicly show an audience that they buy environmentally friendly products because they believe it makes them look good to others. This is never at the expense, however, of their personal comfort and self-interest. Again, a peek behind the curtain will reveal that they don't practice what they preach. Others can sacrifice to save the planet, but not them.

## Marielle: A Communal Narcissist

Marielle is considered to be one of the pillars of her small community. Her sunny disposition and ever-present smile make people overlook her often overly effusive language, both in person and on Facebook. Even when everything is dark and gloomy in the world, Marielle is there to pick everyone up with her positivity.

During the COVID-19 pandemic, while many were losing their jobs and worried about their health (among other things), Marielle would post uplifting messages that were somewhat out of touch with the sense of hopelessness and despair many were feeling: *"Hi Everyone! Everything will be okay!! I am SO proud how our community is coming together in these hard times. I will be volunteering my time delivering food to all our healthcare professionals sacrificing their time for US!! Stay positive! We will get through this TOGETHER!!"*

Positivity is not a bad thing, and we especially need hope and positivity from the leaders of our community. However, Marielle is not a leader of her community, but she likes to act like she is. She sits on many philanthropic boards, regularly volunteers for various causes, and is constantly engaged in efforts to help others. All of these pursuits are enthusiastically posted on her Facebook and Instagram pages. Sharing good deeds, accomplishments, and fundraising for worthy causes is not narcissistic in and of itself, but Marielle doesn't do this because it's simply right to help others. Her motives for this level of involvement are to be showered in praise, which makes her feel like the most important person in town.

Despite her optimistic persona, Marielle is not as full of sunshine, kindness, and positivity as she wants people to believe. She is incredibly condescending and entitled. She makes a big show of buying lavish gifts for people—but only when she thinks she can get something from them. She wants to be seen as "the favorite," particularly by people who she believes can grant her special favors.

Marielle feels entitled and believes she does not have to follow the same rules as other people, stepping all over anyone who stands in her way of getting what she wants. You'd never know this by looking at her social media posts, where she frequently claims to be concerned about those less fortunate. She is also surprisingly catty—to people's faces she is as sweet as pie, but behind their backs, she snickers, rolls her eyes, and exchanges haughty glances with friends, even in public when others are watching.

Marielle does much good in the community—and she will not let you forget it. Social media is the place she can widely broadcast her good deeds, so everyone knows what a good person she is. All Marielle cares about is how she is perceived, but who she really is underneath her façade is far different than the caring, warm, generous person she wants everyone to think she is.

## Collective Narcissism

Collective narcissism is a form of narcissism that, in part, may help to explain some of the most destructive aspects of society, and has possibly contributed to our divisiveness. Collective narcissism can be defined as follows: "a belief that one's own group (the ingroup) is exceptional and entitled to privileged treatment, but it is not sufficiently recognized by others. Thus, central to collective narcissism is resentment that the ingroup's exceptionality is not sufficiently externally appreciated."[27]

Collective narcissism shares many of the same traits of individual narcissism, with the main difference being that the collective narcissist takes offense when they feel the *group* they belong to is under attack, criticized, or undervalued. An individual in a group can be a collective narcissist, but it is also possible that an entire group of people can be collective narcissists, which can result in mass retaliation against individuals or other groups.

Collective narcissism is a threat to peace and safety on a larger scale, as it is tied to hatred, violence, prejudice, and racism. The feeling of the group being underappreciated or devalued results in a hostile reaction from the collective narcissist. The article "Why Collective Narcissists Are So Politically Volatile"[28] explores this and says: "When their own group is involved, collective narcissists have no sense of humor. They are disproportionately punitive in responding to what they perceive as an insult to their group, even when the insult is debatable, not perceived by others, or not intended by the other group. Unlike individual narcissists, collective narcissists cannot dissociate themselves from an unpopular or criticized group. Once their self-worth is invested in the greatness of their group, collective narcissists are motivated by enhancing their group rather than themselves."

The Collective Narcissism Scale (CNS)[29] asks people to first think about the group (this can be any group, from your nationality, to a political party, to a club you belong to) that they identify with when responding to the questions. The scale is from 1 to 6 with one meaning "totally disagree" and 6 meaning "totally agree." The questions are as follows:

- I wish other groups would quickly recognize the authority of my group.
- My group deserves special treatment.
- I will never be satisfied until my group gets the recognition it deserves.
- I insist on my group getting the respect that is due to it. It really makes me angry when others criticize my group.
- If my group had a major say in the world, the world would be a much better place.
- I do not get upset when people do not notice the achievements of my group.
- Not many people seem to fully understand the importance of my group.

• The true worth of my group is often misunderstood.

I interviewed Agnieszka Golec de Zavala, a social psychologist and researcher who is behind much of the major research on collective narcissism, and who created the Collective Narcissism Scale (CNS) above. She told me that you can be narcissistic about any group that is important to you and that collective narcissism happens when we think of ourselves as a group member. These tend to be groups that have realistic existence in society, like nationality, ethnicity, gender, professional groups, and social class.

Golec de Zavala also explained to me that the belief that the group is exceptional happens to both high- and low-status groups. These low-status groups want to feel important but believe their group is not sufficiently recognized by others. She said people who are narcissistic about one type of group are usually narcissistic about other groups with which they identify, and national narcissism and religious narcissism tend to be correlated. So, for instance, if you are collectively narcissistic about the country you are from, you could also have the same narcissism about your religious affiliation. More of Golec de Zavala's fantastic insight will be shared later in this book, in the chapter on racism, politics, and narcissism on social media.

## What Does Collective Narcissism Look Like on Social Media?

Collective narcissism seems to have a distinct presentation on social media. More recently, there has been research on connections between collective narcissism and conspiracy theories. Some collective narcissists use social media to disseminate conspiracy theories online, with Facebook as the social media platform most used for this. Collective narcissists perceive any outside group as a threat to the exceptionality of the in-group, thus perpetuating their belief in conspiracy theories that they believe threaten them.

Collective narcissism has also been linked to nationalism in certain studies. In the article "Nationalism as Collective Narcissism,"[30] it says:

> Traditional conceptualizations of nationalism focus on the need for intergroup domination. We argue that current politics are rather driven by the need for recognition of the greatness of one's nation. In psychological literature, the need for the nation's appreciation is captured by the concept of collective narcissism—a belief in in-group greatness contingent on external recognition. We demonstrate that collective narcissism is associated with support for national populist parties and policies.

With social media posts on platforms like Facebook and Twitter becoming increasingly political and polarized, observing how people post on those websites is probably one of the best insights into their psyche. Social media posts that are tribal in nature are often things people are only comfortable saying online. I have heard countless stories from those who grew to despise old friends, their in-laws, or members of their biological families based on these types of posts. In fact, this morning I received a text from a friend thanking me for telling her how to hide posts from her Facebook feed. It gave her peace of mind to not see the hateful things her family was saying since she couldn't simply "unfriend" them without creating lasting and possibly irreparable rifts.

Social media could also, in part, become a breeding ground for collective narcissism. The digital world allows us to connect with others outside of our immediate circles. While this can be a great thing, groups can gather online to reinforce beliefs of superiority, or even potentially create collective narcissists by drawing people into a group where the person, perhaps for the first time, feels included and special. The sense of belonging to a group for someone who otherwise felt isolated can be intoxicating.

Multiple studies connecting collective narcissism to conspiracy theories, nationalism, and populism, indicate that narcissism is a growing problem that is behind some of the hatred and divisiveness online.

## Brian: From Loneliness and Depression to Conspiracy and Narcissism

Brian started his journey down the conspiracy theory rabbit hole at the age of thirty-two. His father had recently died, only five years after his mother had passed, and the totality of this loss was devastating to him. Brian was already intrigued by conspiracy theories, but, consumed by grief, he began immersing himself in conspiracy theories as a way to distract himself.

Brian joined a small online community and spent all his time corresponding with others in the group. He soon began to feel endangered by anyone outside this circle and was outwardly hostile and cruel to those that he perceived as a threat. He completely bought into the theories being discussed in his group and called those who did not agree with them "stupid" and labeled them as "sheeple."

Brian constantly posted his conspiracy theories online, using threatening language. Most of his followers found the aggressive messaging off-putting and simply scrolled on without replying, which only angered Brian even more. He did not like the feeling of being ignored, especially about the things he deemed as having the utmost importance.

For Brian, the last straw was when his cousin and roommate died in a freak accident. The pain and loneliness were almost unbearable, and he became even more untethered. When he posted the news of the death on his Facebook page, social media friends offered their condolences and sympathy. Instead of finding comfort by their concern, Brian viciously lashed out at them, asking why they ignored all his other important posts but took the time to comment on this.

Brian's story is an example of someone with untreated depression, trauma, and grief, as well as a developing collective narcissist personality on social media. He believed the small online group he identified with was smarter and superior to others outside his group; he was belligerent and aggressive toward others who did not agree with him, and most of this manifested online. He also felt that his group was not recognized for its importance, and he was angry about that.

It could also be argued that social media made him more narcissistic and worsened his anger. Social media was a place that confirmed his biases and where he was able to insulate himself with people that continued to solidify his beliefs, especially when it came to his group. Spewing vitriol and lashing out at others was easy to do hiding behind a keyboard.

## SUMMARY OF THE NARCISSIST SUBTYPES ON SOCIAL MEDIA

As we've discovered, narcissism clearly presents itself in many variations in real life and online and goes far beyond the vanity exhibited by grandiose narcissists. Narcissism is less about vanity and more about lack of empathy, self-centeredness, entitlement, selfishness, exploitation, and the centering of the self or group. While narcissism can be about excessive attention seeking, self-obsession, and vanity, the heart of narcissism is about cruelty and disregard for others.

To succinctly summarize this chapter, here are some key takeaways:

- **Grandiose narcissism** is overt and obvious to most observers. The hallmarks of grandiose narcissism are aggression, extraversion, entitlement, feelings of superiority, hostility, exploitation, and disregard for the feelings and experiences of others.
- **Malignant narcissism** is very dangerous. Malignant narcissists possess traits such as an extreme lack of empathy for

others, a sense of entitlement, and they are exploitative, paranoid, cruel, and sadistic.

- **Vulnerable or covert narcissism** is a more introverted type, while still attention seeking, this subtype is not necessarily grandiose in nature. Shame, neuroticism, hypersensitivity, jealousy, and narcissistic rage are major features of the vulnerable narcissist.

- **Communal narcissism** is what I like to refer to as the "do-gooder" narcissist. This type of narcissist seeks narcissistic supply and feelings of superiority by doing good deeds and by crafting a persona of a "good" and trustworthy person. Communal narcissists are often performative, entitled, and think they are the nicest, best people on the planet. Some may believe they can even change the world with all the good deeds and contributions they make to society. They can also be extremely hypocritical.

- **Collective narcissists** believe that their group (the in-group) is exceptional, entitled to special privileges over other people, and that their group is not recognized for its exceptionality.

# TIPS, TAKEAWAYS, AND FOOD FOR THOUGHT

1. Out of all the subtypes of narcissists discussed in this chapter, do you identify with any of them? Which ones and why? (Remember that it is totally normal to enjoy the feelings of admiration and attention!)

2. How much of your posting on social media is about connecting with others versus posting because you want admiration or attention?

3. Is there anyone in your life who fits any of the descriptions in this chapter? If so, how do you feel when you see their posts? Angry? Frustrated? Annoyed?

4. If you do know anyone that fits these descriptions and they stir up negative feelings, are there ways you can put up boundaries with them on social media? (Example: hide them from your feed, temporarily or indefinitely. Hiding someone from your feed means that they still remain your friend, you just don't see their posts. This may be a better way to do it if you still want to maintain a relationship with this person or if it's not worth it to you to have any bad blood. For others, it may be a better choice to completely remove the person as a friend—especially if you do not care to have a relationship with them anymore.)

# Chapter 2

# ADDICTED TO LIKES: NARCISSISM AND THE BRAIN ON SOCIAL MEDIA

## Lily: It's Not Personal, It's Business

Lily, a thirty-five-year-old entrepreneur and owner of a boutique fitness studio, was initially encouraged to use social media to grow her budding business. Her two young children were finally in school all day, and it presented her with an opportunity to share her love of fitness with her community. She considered herself a free spirit, and although she loved her husband and children, she sometimes resented the constraints and commitments of family life. Lily's husband had suggested starting her business to reclaim parts of her identity that she felt went to the wayside when she became a mother.

Lily's business started to grow as word-of-mouth brought more people to attend classes at the studio. She was encouraged by this and decided that, as the face of the business, she should be a public figure. She hired a social media consultant who told her it might be a good idea to establish a personal brand identity.

In addition to the social media accounts for her studio, Lily created a personal account on Instagram that was public. She used a professional photographer for not only her business account but also for many images on her personal account. It was important to her to have an arsenal of dramatic and attractive photos to post as she pleased. She captioned her photos with her personal learnings, quotes from others, and nuggets of wisdom. She began to fancy herself a teacher and, at times, even a guru.

As her platform slowly grew, so did Lily's sense of self-importance. She enjoyed the feeling of exhilaration she got when notifications of likes and comments lit up her phone. Soon, she became obsessed with posting, mostly about herself because she thought she could be a thought leader. She started to believe she was going to make a huge impact on the world with her knowledge and social media was key to sharing her insights with a large audience. However, if a post did not get as many likes as she had hoped, she would start to feel irritable and depressed. Her husband and kids, who used to be more present on her social media pages, started fading into the background more.

Lily slowly became consumed by a social media addiction that centered around herself and all aspects of her life. To satisfy her cravings for likes and comments, she started to create several other accounts. One was an account she developed as her alter ego so she could express herself more creatively, and she became obsessed with acquiring new followers there as well. Feeding more material to her followers and the euphoric feeling of validation she got when they responded was all-consuming to her, taking precedence over everything else.

Ironically, most of Lily's online teachings were about living in the present, connecting with nature, and fostering relationships. In reality, she was doing the exact opposite. As her social media addiction grew, her relationships became more challenged, her empathy steadily decreased, and the focus on herself became even more extreme.

Eventually, Lily had at least five different Instagram accounts that she spent numerous hours of her life tending to. What started out as a business strategy soon became a massive vanity project. The more self-important she felt through her social media accounts, the more she began to resent anyone or anything that took her away from it—including her family. Her children would make comments to her, saying things like, "Mom, you're always taking pictures," or "Mom you're always on your phone." Her husband grew agitated as well to the point that he blew up at her finally and said if her behavior didn't change, he wanted a divorce. "I have always been a free spirit and you knew this when you married me!" she retorted back.

Unsurprisingly, Lily's marriage continued to disintegrate. She contemplated leaving her husband, but she also knew she needed him to continue the image she portrayed to everyone on social media. Eventually Lily and her husband agreed to go to counseling for the sake of the children, but Lily also knew that keeping the family together was a part of her image, and she also realized she could use the marital problems to gain more followers. Lily, using her excuse that as a free spirit she was wildly vulnerable, convinced her husband to let her post about their counseling journey together.

Even more troubling, Lily also posted misinformation that was potentially dangerous and harmful for those who blindly followed her. She was a staunch believer in natural healing to the extent that she told people to stop taking lifesaving medications prescribed by their physicians, including chemotherapy for cancer patients. Lily became more unhinged and dogmatic as time went on, acting like a doctor when it was clear she had no medical degree or training in medicine.

While Lily's story is not necessarily unique in the digital age, and many of us are well-aware of the dangers of becoming too reliant on social media, the connections that social media addiction have with narcissism have not been fully explored. As I write this, we are still entrenched in the first global pandemic of many of our lifetimes, forcing people to socially distance from each other and live a large portion of their lives online. People are working from home, many children have spent a big chunk of their childhood in virtual school, meetings have been shifted to Zoom, and many of us have relied on social media platforms and technology for human connection.

The Harris Poll conducted a survey between March and early May 2020 and found that between 46 and 51 percent of US adults were using social media more than before the pandemic.[31] As a mental health professional and someone who specializes in healthy relationships, I am very interested in how our increasing reliance on digital platforms, and specifically social media, is impacting our relationships and how we live our lives. Now that the pandemic has forced many of our social interactions from in-person to online, at least for a significant period of time, I wonder how long we will feel the implications from this?

Because narcissism (and not necessarily the personality disorder NPD) is something I believe is an underlying destructive force in relationships on an individual, community, and global level, I believe that an overreliance on technology and social media can exacerbate or even create some narcissistic tendencies.

The pandemic may not only fuel a mental health crisis but may have other consequences, such as increasing narcissism, due to all the time spent online. Anger, frustration, and resentment are results of this pandemic, often because of all the restrictions. Those feelings can easily turn into entitlement and lack of empathy for others. It takes a large amount of self-awareness to not center ourselves and our needs in times of crisis and to act for a collective benefit, but it's important that communities work together for the benefit of all.

Social media has proven to be addictive and often harmful if it starts to become an overwhelming force in our lives. There have been numerous studies on the brain and social media and how we literally feel rewarded when we hear the infamous ping or that steady stream of notifications lighting up our devices. Perhaps the most intoxicating aspect that our brain responds to as it relates to social media is the "high" people feel when they receive likes and comments on social media posts.

In "Your Brain on Facebook,"[32] an article in *Harvard Business Review*, David Rock highlights that the human brain's favorite pastime is to think about people and that social rewards light up the brain's reward circuit more than non-social rewards. Human beings crave positive social interactions, in part, because our brain does this, and we feel good when we experience authentic connection with others. Furthermore, the article states:

> The circuitry activated when you connect online is the seeking circuitry of dopamine. Yet when we connect with people online, we don't tend to get the oxytocin or serotonin calming reward that happens when we bond with someone in real time, when our circuits resonate with real-time shared emotions and experiences. On Twitter, you won't feel satisfied the way you might if you chatted in person with fifty people at a conference. An overabundance of dopamine—while it feels great, just as sugar does—creates a mental hyperactivity that reduces the capacity for deeper focus.

This quote explains why the rewards we receive in our brain from social media are so fleeting. It is not necessarily meaningful connection, but we are getting the dopamine that leaves us wanting more, yet still left feeling strangely empty. The hallmarks of narcissism, as discussed in prior chapters, are low empathy, entitlement, and exploitation. If we are not getting the benefits of true bonding from social media that we get from in-person interactions, then we are not necessarily experiencing empathic connection with others, and in many cases, our empathy reduces online when we cannot meaningfully connect with another person.

In sessions with my clients, I often remind them to have important discussions in person as opposed to over phone, text, or e-mail. While something like Facetiming can be better, in-person human connection is far superior when cultivating empathy. It's so important to see someone's facial cues, eyes, and body language to foster something as important as empathy.

Emiliana Simon-Thomas, science director at the University of California Berkeley's Greater Good Science Center, says that (with social media):

> People get worse at "reading" each other's emotional expressions. When we can't read each other to begin with, we erode our ability to connect, and our overall health and well-being.[33]

With low levels of empathy, we cannot have close and connected relationships that bring us joy. As numerous studies have found over the years, it is the quality, not quantity of relationships that brings people true happiness.[34] As empathy lessens, it is only inevitable that narcissism would increase. The focus becomes more about the self than the connection with another person.

What about addiction to likes and comments on social media? How does that aspect of social media addiction contribute to fueling narcissism? If we are constantly preoccupied with talking about ourselves, presenting ourselves in a certain light, and relying on responses and reinforcement from the cyberworld to make us feel good about ourselves, it encourages a preoccupation of the self and a false sense of importance. Narcissism is often about the need to feel important and special, although one does not have to have a high self-esteem to be a narcissist. In fact, narcissists are often thought to have a low self-esteem and deep feelings of insecurity and inferiority. The inflated sense of self-worth is thought only to be a defense mechanism to cover feelings of inadequacy. Likes and comments are a superficial and external way to gain validation, which would be quite intoxicating for someone with narcissistic tendencies.

Even if one did not initially have narcissistic tendencies, an addiction to validation through likes and comments could certainly encourage narcissistic behaviors. If we get a lot of thumbs-ups on a photo or a post, it is only normal to feel special. The more we believe people are interested in every mundane aspect of our lives, and the more addicted we become to sharing those minor details (in many cases with people we do not know well), we may start to feel an exaggerated sense of self-importance.

It is only human to want to feel special and validation is important. However, it becomes unhealthy when we become addicted to feeling special and go to great lengths to get that validation. If our self-worth is dictated by how others respond to us on social media, then when they do not respond in the way we want them to, that can cause feelings of despair, emptiness, and depression.

I equate the addiction to likes and comments on social media, and the negative feelings associated with the lack of them, to the concepts of narcissistic supply and narcissistic rage. Likes and comments can be a form of narcissistic supply. True narcissists are addicted to narcissistic supply and use any means necessary to get it. They thrive off of narcissistic supply and rely on it to keep them feeling important and superior. A person who is not very narcissistic may be lured by the reward system activated in the brain every time they are validated online. If you are getting rewarded all the time in a way that makes you feel special, you may gradually start to believe you are, but only based on external factors that are superficial and unsatisfying in the long-term.

Lily, the boutique fitness center owner who felt compelled to open multiple social media accounts, is an example of a growing social media addiction that fueled her narcissistic tendencies. Lily could switch back and forth between accounts and almost always find some form of validation from all the posting and sharing she was doing.

Narcissistic rage stemming from social media addiction can be triggered when a person believes they are not getting the amount of validation they crave or believe they deserve. Lily would become angry and irritable if she felt her posts were not getting enough recognition. The feelings of shame, inadequacy, and anger that happen for some people when they feel dismissed online can provoke a response of lashing out or even coldly withdrawing.

The human brain perceives social threats and threats to social status in the same way it perceives physical pain.[35] Social media is a place we find social threats that would not have been there otherwise. People feel left out when they see photos of events or parties they were not invited to, and they may also feel a sense of threat to the self if they feel ignored or invalidated on a social media platform. Because the brain's response to social threat is so emotionally painful, it's no wonder social media can make even the most seemingly secure person feel self-doubt. The same goes for the social rewards from social media. If the brain is experiencing something pleasurable when we are given positive attention online, anyone could be lured into the enticing world of constant oversharing and self-absorption.

## THE NPD BRAIN ON SOCIAL MEDIA

While the brain's response to social media revolves around the experiences of pleasure and pain and potentially predisposes people to acquiring some narcissistic tendencies, imagine how powerful the response to social media would be in someone high on the spectrum of narcissism, or clinically diagnosed with narcissistic personality disorder. Because of research, we now know that people who are highly narcissistic post more selfies[36] and post more often than those who are not narcissistic.[37] There is even a study that suggests that narcissistic people find a "happy hunting ground for their narcissistic needs" on social media. This particular study infers "that validation through 'likes' on a real 'selfie' posted online reduced neural indices of emotional arousal after social exclusion." This means that validation from social media can actually *reduce* the distress that a narcissist feels after feeling socially excluded. Perhaps a narcissist would be even more inclined to become addicted to social media because the reward of validation is of the utmost importance to them.

## POWER, EXPLOITATION, AND ENTITLEMENT ON SOCIAL MEDIA

A narcissist will use social media to fill a need for the more deviant traits of the disorder, such as exploitation, entitlement, and urge for power and control. A malignant narcissist with a sadistic streak will feed off seeing others in pain and will even enjoy it. Social media is the perfect medium for a narcissist to exploit others, act entitled, or seek power over others. An interesting study that looked at motivating factors for college students using Instagram in relation to narcissism found a positive correlation between narcissism and those who were motivated to use Instagram to be cool or for "surveillance" (knowledge about others). While curiosity about others (or in social media terms, going into a "black hole" and emerging yourself in someone else's page) does not have anything to do with narcissism; narcissistic individuals will use surveillance and knowledge of others to compete, or target others.

Narcissists using social media may use entitled status updates as an attempt to feel powerful. For example, a narcissist may proclaim they are deleting followers and doing a mass purge. They may even use statements like *"Watch out! You might be next!"* Feeling powerful and entitled and exploiting others can feed their urge for narcissistic supply, and an addiction to social media may reward these insidious desires.

Even those who are not pathological narcissists may use social media and come across as entitled, which gives them a sense of power and feeling of control in their lives. Anxiety is having the feeling of being out of control, and for some, feeling in control and having a sense of power over others is addicting. Dangerous and malignant narcissism involves the enjoyment of power, control, and exploitation of others and, in some cases, the high that comes with all of it.

There are those who are insecure and anxious, and they may give that vibe on social media, but they do not enjoy hurting or seeing others in pain. That is an important distinction to make between a true narcissist and someone who may on occasion engage in behaviors that are part of the profile of a clinical narcissist.

It is easy to see how someone like Lily was able to develop narcissistic traits through her excessive use of social media that ultimately turned into addiction. It is now widely known and accepted (highlighted by the popular documentary *The Social Dilemma*) that platforms like Facebook were designed to addict us, despite the consequences to society. One of those consequences is not just deterioration of mental health but the increase of self-absorption, vanity, and narcissistic traits. Dangerous narcissists use social media as a playground—a place where their cruelty can run amok. Not only do they use social media as a tool to exploit others for personal gain, to taunt, bully, and get their narcissistic supply, but they are also rewarded from the experience because of the way social media is designed.

A narcissist addicted to social media has the potential to inflict great damage on others. Not only do we need to learn how to protect ourselves from the narcissists of the world, but we need to protect ourselves from the narcissists that lurk in cyberspace. Most of us recognize that social media can make us feel bad, but we do not realize that much of what makes us feel bad is tied to dealing with narcissists or witnessing narcissism on these platforms. Even those of us with the best of intentions need to be fully aware of when too much social media starts to push us into becoming more narcissistic so we can step back and reconnect with what is most important to us—our human relationships and our empathy.

You may be thinking that it makes sense to learn how to protect ourselves and our loved ones from the most predatory types of narcissists on social networking websites, but why might I need to protect myself from someone like Lily—a seemingly harmless woman? The issue is not necessarily Lily as an individual problem, but more so, all the collective Lilies on social media. If the addictive nature of social media is contributing to a culture of narcissism, then this is bad news for the future.

President Teddy Roosevelt famously said, "Comparison is the thief of joy." The fact that social media can disconnect us from real connection[39] and the emptiness that comes from a quick fix of validation that crashes down shortly thereafter are a few reasons why it feels toxic to many people. If we have a culture where people make it their mission to create and curate an unrealistic life online, and then we come to rely on social networking to define our success and self-worth, we are falling into a dangerous trap of a disingenuous, shallow, and narcissistic world, one where the focus on self, often at the expense of others and the collective good, is the priority. Is this what we want for our children: a society where they no longer aspire to be artists, musicians, astronauts, teachers, and doctors who are connected members of their communities but instead influencers collecting subscribers and likes from people with whom they'll never have a real conversation? I think not.

Again, it all makes sense that affirmation and validation feel good to us. It also makes sense that so many of us want to feel special and important. Human beings need love, affirmation, and appreciation, and there is nothing wrong with that. Especially if we did not get these things in childhood, we crave them desperately. As mentioned earlier, attention-seeking behaviors can be a response to trauma.

Historically, for survival, human beings needed to show their group that they were a valued member who could contribute, and this is one reason the need to feel respected and appreciated is deeply ingrained in our brains. As Dr. Joseph Shrand stated in an article in *Psychology Today*:

> This survival mode explains why I get angry, anxious, or sad when I feel less valued. The limbic part of my brain worries I may get kicked out of my protective group and be easier prey. Right or wrong, just the perception of being devalued activates our ancient, irrational, emotional, and impulsive limbic response.[40]

Beyond that, humans are simply wired for connection. We are relational creatures. Babies are born helpless and need their mothers (or another attentive primary caregiver) to survive. Humans form groups and live in communities together to enhance their well-being. This may be for more than just evolutionary survival. Human connection is bigger than all of us and beyond what we can really understand. Love is a driving force for all that is good. Love, connection, empathy . . . these are all characteristics that are the opposite of narcissism. In the last chapter of this book, I will explore some potential solutions to use social media for purposes that are the opposite of narcissism. Social media and its addictive nature are not going anywhere, but we can hopefully learn to use some aspects of it for good.

## TIPS, TAKEAWAYS, AND FOOD FOR THOUGHT

1. How do you feel when you get a lot of "likes" on a social media post?
2. How do you feel when something you post is not acknowledged? Write down some of your feelings and the stories you make up about that (e.g., I feel disappointed and angry and the story I make up is that no one cares about me).
3. Next time you feel upset or happy related to validation you did or did not receive on a social media post, notice what you are feeling and try to let it pass. What would it be like to not be affected by positive or negative validation?

# Chapter 3

# NOT EVERYTHING IS WHAT IT SEEMS: NARCISSISM AND FALSE NARRATIVES ON SOCIAL MEDIA

Years ago, I had a personal Facebook account. The initial months of my experience with social networking were exciting as I reconnected with people from all different chapters of my life. With a click of the mouse, Facebook allowed me to quickly find some of my childhood schoolmates and best friends from the years I lived in England as a little girl. Before the existence of the platform, this would have taken tremendous detective-like sleuthing. Thanks to Facebook, I reunited with them in person a few years ago, right before the pandemic began. We hugged and cried tears of joy in a moment I'll never forget. Even though twenty years had passed since we had seen each other, it was like nothing had changed.

Relationships are of the utmost importance to me. Many of my closest friendships are from childhood and college, and I have friends from different times in my life that I work hard to keep up with. Initially, Facebook was a great way to stay connected.

Like most shiny new toys, my love affair with Facebook soon tarnished. However, I stuck with it for years because I found it easier to keep up with people who didn't live close by and was worried we would lose touch. Eventually, my "friend" list soon crept up to over 700 people. My mind had a hard time wrapping around this fact because, obviously, I didn't have this many *real friends.* When I posted a few pictures of my firstborn child in 2012, I wondered, *Do most of these people even care?* Likely not casual acquaintances or someone I met once in Jamaica five years ago, even if they randomly click a thumbs-up. The only people who really want to see photos of my children and all the cute things they are doing are family and close friends. Other questions crept into my mind. *Are the people outside those categories getting a voyeuristic glimpse into my life? How many people do I even want to look into a window of my personal life?*

Along with my personal fears, what started to chip away at me most was the constant portrayal of the picture-perfect life in my newsfeed, the excessive over-posting and over-sharing, and of course, the constant bragging that seemed to clog my feed.

To be honest and fair, I was probably guilty of all these things at one point or another. Just like anyone else, I can be easily sucked into the attraction of social media—and its addictive tendencies. However, I didn't like when I felt myself doing those things that some might find annoying—it did not feel good or authentic in any way.

I certainly don't expect people to air their dirty laundry and life crises online for all to see, particularly when most connections are usually just acquaintances. Do you really want Jane, that woman you said "hi" to in the hall in high school back in 1997, to know all about your divorce? Likely not. But what does puzzle and fascinate me about the phenomenon of social media is the complete opposite portrayal of one's life versus the reality of it.

At the height of my social media use, my Facebook friends all knew I was a therapist-in-training, which eventually changed to licensed psychotherapist. At that time in my life, I clearly remember the posts of an acquaintance of mine, Valerie. She was a lovely person—sweet, kind, bubbly, and always smiling. She was also an over-the-top, annoying oversharer. It got to a point where mutual friends would comment to me that her posts made them cringe. Valerie was obsessed with her husband, posting several times a day about how great he was and how amazing their relationship was. People were genuinely happy that Valerie seemed to have found the great love of her life—but did anyone want to see or hear about it multiple times a day? Definitely not! She seemed self-centered and oblivious, and people started to hide her posts from their newsfeed.

I'd only known Valerie through mutual friends, so I was surprised to receive a message from her one day asking to get coffee. I agreed, and we met one afternoon. After casual conversation, she began to cry. She told me some awful things about her marriage and her husband, who she said was abusive to her. I was shocked because it was exactly the opposite of what she showed the world on social media.

"Wow. I'm just so surprised to hear that because everything seemed so great from what you've been sharing on Facebook," I told her.

"Not everything is what it seems," she told me.

This was not the last time this happened while I was on Facebook.

Because I am a couples therapist, I regularly received messages from people asking me for recommendations for marriage counseling and often confiding in me when things were in shambles. More often than not, these were the very same people who were posting the most effusive things about their lives and their partners.

Why do people create false narratives like this? It is one thing to pretend everything is fine, but it's another to go to great lengths to convince people of something that is false. Perhaps it is partly to do with defense mechanisms. We want to protect ourselves from feeling the pain of our reality, so we go through a mix of denial and reaction formation. Reaction formation is when someone reacts or acts in opposite ways of how they truly feel. If we can convince others that our life is picture-perfect, maybe we can convince ourselves, too. Or maybe it feels good, even for a moment, to pretend that everything is great when it is deeply painful.

When people post obsessively about their lives, others seem to judge that behavior as narcissistic. While that assessment is not entirely false, and those people certainly can be narcissists, it also does not mean that they are. However, it is worth noting that research shows strong evidence that not only are high levels of Facebook use associated with narcissism, but a study from Germany also found that anxiety is the strongest predictor of Facebook addiction.[41] What is even more fascinating about this study is that vulnerable (or covert) narcissism was a greater predictor of social media addiction than grandiose narcissism.

The stakes are high on social media for vulnerable and grandiose narcissists. The German study explains why vulnerable narcissists are not just attracted to posting on social media, but also extremely addicted to it:

> Because of their enhanced defensiveness and low social competence, vulnerable narcissists are typically not able to promote a positive image of their person in face-to-face social interactions. Consequently, their strong need for attention and admiration remains unsatisfied. On Facebook, they have enough time to create and control their social interactions and self-presentation. This condition increases the probability to receive positive feedback from other users and thus to compensate its lack in the offline world.

The incentive for people with narcissistic traits and disordered narcissists to create false narratives on social media is high, and they may spend a lot of time curating what appears to be the perfect life to gain attention and admiration.

## Scarlet: Stage-Mommy Dearest

Scarlet could be described as a stage mom of sorts. She is a forty-three-year-old stay-at-home mom who went to business school but preferred to stay home instead of working so she could focus on her children. Her eleven-year-old daughter Jessie is a talented ballet dancer, and Scarlet has pushed her to dance as soon as Jessie was able to walk. Jessie does not love ballet, but she does it because her mother wants her to, and the only way Jessie gets any love or warmth from her mother is when she is doing what Scarlet wants. When Jessie performs well, her mother takes to social media to brag and then pushes her daughter to do more. But if Jessie disappoints her mother or does not live up to her standards, she is punished or ignored. Jessie does not know which is worse, as they both feel awful to her.

Scarlet also has a seven-year-old son, Austin, who she essentially casts to the side like an afterthought. Scarlet only wanted daughters, and because she is a narcissist and only cares about herself and her image, she is resentful that Austin was not another daughter she could parade around on the stage. Scarlet's husband, Dominic, is the quintessential nice guy. Some would even go so far as to say he's a doormat. Scarlet verbally berates him and emotionally abuses him daily. She snaps at him, criticizes him, orders him around, and when he does not do what she wants, she gives him the silent treatment for days on end. Scarlet's pride and joy are not her children but her two Samoyed dogs, Buffy and Muffy. They are spotless, white, beautiful purebreds, and Scarlet dotes on them more than any human in her family.

Scarlet is an example of a grandiose narcissist addicted to social media and the narcissistic supply it brings her. Scarlet's friend Amy started to notice something was off when she observed not only the self-serving grandiose social media posts that Scarlet was frequently sharing but the major discrepancies between what she shared online versus the real story behind closed doors.

When Amy first became friendly with Scarlet, she noticed Scarlet would obsessively post about her dogs and rarely post about her children. She especially never posted anything about her son Austin, and Jessie was only mentioned if she did well in a ballet recital or was posing with the dogs. Amy began to feel uncomfortable when Scarlet started to insert subtle snide remarks about Jessie's ballet performances online. She would critique her daughter's performance for all to see in a way that was shaming. Jessie may or may not have seen those posts, but it was a violation of boundaries nonetheless.

Amy got to experience the real Scarlet when she witnessed her unleash a verbal tirade at Dominic that made her jaw drop. This was a far cry from Scarlet's posts calling him "the best husband ever," followed by over-the-top praise detailed in a multiple-paragraph declaration of devotion. Scarlet was intent on creating a false narrative of domestic bliss when her family situation was exactly the opposite.

Scarlet is consumed by keeping up appearances that she has a great life and posts three to four times daily to make sure no one misses anything. In addition to her grandiosity, she also has some traits of the communal narcissist. Any time she donates to a worthy cause, she stands on her virtual soapbox with lengthy posts about all her charitable contributions inferring what a generous and honorable person she is. She would never consider giving for giving's sake—all her good deeds are to reap narcissistic supply.

# Sandra: Living the False Life

Sandra has narcissistic traits, but unlike Scarlet, her traits are more in line with the vulnerable/covert narcissistic profile in person, though her social media persona is grandiose. Sandra and her husband are very much "keeping up with the Joneses" and flaunt their wealth online any chance they get. They come across as gauche to others, posting excessively about their expensive cars, luxurious vacations, and staged, professional photos of their children in designer clothing.

Those who only knew Sandra online would be surprised to find that, if they met her in person, she is actually shy and self-conscious. It's as if social media has given Sandra an alter ego—one who is showy and a braggart.

Sandra is excessively insecure, defensive, and hypersensitive to anything she perceives as criticism. Social media is a place where she can alleviate some of the anxiety around her insecurities. She takes great care curating her posts and strives to portray her life like the bevy of influencers she sees with flawless images. Because of Sandra's insecurities, and because she grew up poor as the daughter of a mother obsessed with achieving social status, her social media displays are to let people know that she is important and of a high social stature.

Most people in Sandra's social circles find her posts insufferable, cringing to themselves every time she strikes a pose with "duck lips" and crossing one leg in front of the other with a pointed toe. Sandra is oblivious to how others perceive her. Instead of people being envious of her life, they are judging it and often even mocking her.

While the lavish experiences and luxury goods are real, Sandra's life behind the scenes is far from happy. Her husband is cruel and belittling, and he is likely a grandiose narcissist. Her three children are in and out of therapy for various behavioral issues, which is not surprising considering they are used as props and pushed to overachieve and excel at everything. They are not allowed to be tired or upset, and if they behave in a way their father deems as inappropriate, they are mocked, berated, and punished. Sandra goes along with all of it because her husband is wealthy and also a vital part of her image and appearance. It is why she married him in the first place. He was a trophy to her and made her look good, despite his ugly qualities on the inside. Because she is so deeply insecure, having the trophy husband makes her feel that she is special by association.

There are many examples of how vulnerable, communal, and grandiose narcissists spend countless hours creating an alternate reality about themselves and their lives. They want everyone to think that they are perfect, and they want you to think their spouses, children, and lives are perfect as well. They want you to envy them, and they thrive off the attention they receive from social media.

Why is the creation of an exaggerated false life on social media, especially one that is designed to induce envy in friends and followers, problematic? The issue is not that one is simply trying to portray their best life; it is about the toxic and narcissistic behavior that is contributing to a larger mental health crisis. Prior to the COVID-19 global pandemic, one in ten adults in the US reported symptoms of anxiety and depression, and one in five reported symptoms of any mental illness.[42] During the pandemic, many people experienced worsened symptoms or depression, anxiety, and trauma for the first time. The long-term impacts of the pandemic will be felt for years to come, especially for those who dealt with job loss, food and economic insecurity, and isolation. Those with prior health issues and pre-existing illness that made them high risk for contracting the virus, frontline and essential workers, and communities of color were disproportionately impacted by the devastating effects of the pandemic.

If people with narcissistic traits and diagnosable narcissists are the more frequent offenders of not only posting with higher frequency but also consistently portraying a false picture-perfect image online, then that will only perpetuate an already existing mental health crisis. This is one of many reasons why narcissistic people can be so damaging to those around them. So many people already compare themselves to others and feel bad after they do so. Narcissists want you to compare your life to theirs and then feel bad about your life. It makes these narcissistic types feel powerful and in control. They want to be better than you, often because their insecurities are so deep.

Even nice people like Valerie, with the best of intentions, contribute to making others feel bad about themselves by posting an idyllic fairy-tale life that is exactly the opposite of the truth. Nicky Lidbetter, the CEO of Anxiety UK, says:

> When people start to compare themselves to what they are seeing on social media, they can find themselves trying to meet unrealistic expectations, leading to increased self-doubt, body image insecurity, feelings of anxiety and lowered self-esteem.[42]

The fact is, no one has a perfect life, and false expectations of what we think life should be and should look like can lead to anxiety, depression, and feelings of low self-worth. Alain de Botton, a philosopher and author, says, in reference to the messages society dictates to us:

> An ordinary life is not good enough . . . you need to be extraordinary. Become Mark Zuckerberg. Become somebody else. This is a kind of torture that we've imposed on ourselves. How have we made a life where the statistical odds of you leading that life . . . the 99 percent surety that you will lead that life has come to seem like a humiliation and the wrong sort of life?[43]

Alain de Botton is right, and social media is perpetuating the idea that all that is worth showing is an extraordinary life that is enviable. It's alarming to think that so many are encouraged, at least subconsciously, to promote materialism and self-worth based on how many people are watching you and consuming your content. Nothing is wrong with living an "ordinary" or "mediocre" life. Life is mostly filled with mundane moments, and true happiness is about finding contentment instead of always looking for the next best thing.

This narrative often presents itself as *"if only"* thinking. This is when we believe we would be happier *"if only"* we had something else or more than what we already have. It becomes a vicious, repetitive cycle in our minds, and we are never content or happy because there is always more to acquire, more to achieve, more to gain.

Humans tend to put their energy into what is wrong instead of what is right. If 90 percent of your life is going well, it is only natural you would want to focus on the 10 percent that is not going well. That 10 percent of strife is uncomfortable and gnaws at us, and we want to fix whatever we think is wrong so we can feel 100 percent whole.

Philosophers, scientists, and the world's major religions all examine happiness and contentment and its connectivity to being happy with what you have instead of focusing on what you do not have. Altruism and giving back to others with the purpose of making someone else happy or contributing to their well-being has also been linked to happiness.[44] This type of altruism, which comes from a good place and not a self-serving one, is the opposite of narcissism. I believe that the major forces opposing narcissism are contentment with self, empathy for others, and altruism.

Of course, we cannot talk about happiness without a dose of realism. Happiness is not just something we can magically experience if we wake up one day and just decide to find contentment in the mundane. Genetics, brain chemistry, privilege, and external events outside of our control (grief and trauma symptoms) all play a role in whether someone is happy or content. Therefore, when narcissism, entitlement, self-centeredness, and materialism are constantly in our social media newsfeeds, they can contribute to chipping away at our mental health. False narratives on social media can take someone who is already fragile mentally and push them over the edge.

What if you feel that you are posting more than you should or are conscious that you are posting—sometimes creating false narratives—to seek attention and validation? First, it's an amazing thing to have the self-awareness to recognize that some of your social media habits may be unhealthy for you and others around you. Hopefully, this book will help you understand some of the motivations around this, and you may experience some deeper reflections and insights into your online behavior and what aspects of it that may be worth changing.

Secondly, just because you enjoy posting about your life frequently and are aware that the validation of likes feels good, or even addicting, it does not mean you are a narcissist or have narcissistic traits! It is normal and perfectly fine to want to share your joys, your successes, and your happiness with your loved ones, and it is normal to enjoy the feeling of validation when you are appreciated. You should decide for yourself whether your social media use is problematic, and if you don't feel it is causing any problems in your life and that it only contributes to your happiness, then that's a great thing!

False narratives, narcissism, and narcissists on social media are not magically going to go away, so what are some things we can do to help mitigate the bad feelings that arise when we compare ourselves to others on social media, often because we imagine they are doing so much better than we are in life? The stories in the case studies are clear examples of how much social media narratives distort reality. It is important to stop and recognize that what is presented on social media is not necessarily the truth or the whole picture. In fact, many times it is the opposite of the truth, as we've learned.

We can also recognize that often the people boasting the most or portraying the most idyllic lives on social media could be narcissists, have narcissistic traits, or are possibly dealing with anxiety, trauma, grief, or pain.

Either way, at the end of the day, many of these posts and false narratives are coming from a place of insecurity and unhappiness. People who are content and happy with their lives do not feel the need to constantly share them, especially with the intention of wanting to make other people envious. While people who are narcissists or slightly narcissistic may be getting some gratification, validation, and a hit of narcissistic supply, it's all short-lived.

Instead of focusing on or longing for what other people appear to have, start to think about your own goals that are unique to you and how you can achieve them. Cultivating gratitude is another important way to put the focus back on being content with what you already have. If comparing yourself to others on social media is often too overwhelming or is really taking a toll on your mental health, then it may be important to reach out and seek help from a mental health professional. If the comparison to others feels all-consuming and is making you feel sad or anxious, or if you have trouble disconnecting from social media, professional help may be needed. Following are some tips and exercises to help you explore how narcissism and false narratives on social media may be playing a part in your life.

# TIPS, TAKEAWAYS, AND FOOD FOR THOUGHT

1. How often do you post on social media? Does it feel gratifying? Does it feel empty? Something else?
2. Do you like to portray a life of perfection or something that is not quite the truth about how you feel about your life? If so, what are your motivations for wanting others to see your life in a certain way?
3. How do you feel looking at other people's lives on your social media feeds? Do you find yourself comparing yourself to others a lot? How does that make you feel?
4. Cultivate gratitude by taking the time every night to write (or think about) all the things you are grateful for that you currently have. Try doing this as soon as you wake up in the morning as well.
5. If the constant scrolling through social media feeds and comparing yourself to others takes its toll on you, consider a social media "detox." That can mean taking a break from social media for a few days to a few weeks to indefinitely.

# Chapter 4

# RISE OF THE INFLUENCER: HOW SOCIAL MEDIA IS ENHANCING CULTURAL NARCISSISM THROUGH CELEBRITY

## Heather: Don't Hate Me Because I'm Fabulous

Even before the emergence of social media, Heather was histrionic and narcissistic. One of the defining features of histrionic personality disorder (HPD) is that people with it "use their physical appearance, acting in inappropriately seductive or provocative ways, to gain the attention of others. They lack a sense of self-direction and are highly suggestible, often acting submissively to retain the attention of others."[45]

Heather displays classic histrionic behavior: she needs to be the center of attention at all times and hates when she isn't. She uses her physical appearance to get attention from others, only has shallow emotions, and is overtly sexual and provocative. She also has narcissistic tendencies: she craves narcissistic supply and uses other people to get what she wants.

When Heather first became aware of Instagram influencers, she decided this was the perfect job for her. She always wanted to be famous, she just did not know how she was going to get there. She was never interested in acting and she did not have any musical talent. She had once dabbled with the idea of auditioning for a reality television show, but being an influencer sounded like a much faster and easier way to launch her to fame and fortune. It seemed that all anyone needed to be an influencer was the will, the patience, and the ability to market themselves.

Heather was determined to make this idea work. She paid for tens of thousands of followers on Instagram—many were bots—and soon she was able to grow her "audience" to over 100,000 followers. Heather posted content all day, centering herself in wild and provocative clothing, often in tiny bikinis and lingerie. Heather started getting some attention on her social media page and was soon asked to promote certain products, even giving followers her own code for discounts.

Heather was convinced she had finally made it. What she didn't take into account is that influencers still have to maintain some sense of *connection* to others, even online. Heather was so self-centered and shallow that she frequently made offensive comments and was shockingly insensitive to other people and their circumstances. When the coronavirus pandemic hit, with many people struggling to put food on the table after losing their jobs, Heather continued to post provocative photos of herself at luxurious five-star resorts, saying, "I don't care what's going on in the world. Fun is still on my agenda." When her followers called her out for being "tone deaf," she doubled down and got angry with them, saying, "Haters gonna hate. Sorry, losers, I have a life to live!"

While her tone-deaf posts were maddening, what was truly disturbing was her next step in gaining attention. Heather realized that her young daughters, ages four and five, could also benefit from her platform, so she started posting pictures of them—with full makeup and provocative dress, like the young beauty pageant contestants that became so controversial—with no consideration of the dangerous consequences from child predators of this kind of exploitation. Heather's page lit up with messages from people concerned about what she was doing to her children, but Heather just scoffed at them: "MYOB. Sorry your girls aren't beautiful enough to post!"

There is no clear mission for Heather's page other than grandiose exhibitionism. Nothing and no one—not even the safety of her children—is going to stop her.

## INFLUENCING AND NARCISSISM

Most influencers have some sort of niche theme that ranges from the expected and sometimes useful—fashion, makeup, hairstyling, housecleaning, social activism—to the head-scratching, such as "mukbang," where people show live videos of themselves eating large amounts of food. You name it, and there is a social media influencer for any genre. Anyone seeking fame in any capacity can give it a go. You don't need a talent to be famous anymore, and this has never been more evident than with the rise of reality television and social media platforms like TikTok. All you need to do is act in an unusual or extreme way and cause drama. Reality television explicitly and implicitly tells us that drama sells, and of course it does. People watch reality television specifically, if not solely, for the drama—the fights, the backstabbing, the failures.

One could say marketing and self-promotion are talents in their own right, especially if you can make a decent living doing them. Social media has encouraged a world filled with marketing, advertising, self-branding, and self-promotion. Unfortunately, the overconsumption of these things gives the wrong message and contributes to a narcissistic society focused mainly on individualism, consumerism, and capitalism. An individual engaging in marketing, advertising, self-promotion, and self-branding isn't necessarily narcissistic (although they can be). However, the constant bombardment of these things is not a good thing for society and its relationship to narcissism.

Currently, there is immense pressure to use social media to promote anything and everything, especially ourselves. There is nothing wrong with promoting yourself and sharing your accomplishments, and it can be inspiring for others to hear success stories from others, but when the promotion and branding become excessive, we can become self-focused at the expense of everything else in life. If we engage in this self-focus often enough, it has the potential to chip away at our empathy, give us a sense of entitlement, and can contribute to the exploitation of innocent people for our personal gain, all of which is heading straight toward narcissism territory.

We live in a society driven by money and success—defined as being famous or rich. To keep up with the rat race, many of us feel forced into a space that we are uncomfortable with or that makes us feel inadequate if we are not meeting society's demands of what our success should look like. We are flooded with messages that tell us if we look a certain way, make a certain amount of money, have a ton of followers on social media, and hang around powerful people, then we must be important and worthy.

What no one tells us is that often the path to becoming powerful, famous, and wealthy requires a certain amount of ruthlessness. Sometimes, fame, fortune, and power are built on a foundation of deceit. Getting to the top of the ladder of social hierarchy can mean exploiting others for personal gain, losing empathy, and acting entitled. In other words, the type of success we are conditioned to achieve may involve destructive narcissism. People like Bernie Madoff, Jeffrey Epstein, and Harvey Weinstein are just a few examples of some of the most psychopathic and narcissistic people who were once at the very top of their game.

Social media offers a dangerous combination of addiction and narcissistic supply to people who are already seeking some form of fame and notoriety as a public figure. W. Keith Campbell, professor, researcher, author, and expert on narcissism, tells me:

> If you're focused on other people or fame, you're screwed. Fame is fleeting. That's the nature of fame. Even legit famous people, they get famous, it goes away, they are hungry for it the rest of their life. That's the nature of it. It's a bad strategy for having a good life.

# INFLUENCERS, ADDICTION, AND THE INCREASE OF NARCISSISM

Some research points to the idea that excessive social media use can increase narcissistic tendencies. Influencers and social media mavens are encouraged to post regularly to drive engagement, so what might the consequences be for someone who makes it a career to use social media all the time? In a study from Swansea University and Milan University,[46] researchers looked at personality changes over a four-month period while assessing participants' usage of social media. Those who used social media excessively, through visual postings, displayed an average 25 percent increase in such narcissistic traits over the four months of the study. Professor Phil Reed from the Department of Psychology at Swansea University and who led the study, said:

> There have been suggestions of links between narcissism and the use of visual postings on social media, such as Facebook, but, until this study, it was not known if narcissists use this form of social media more, or whether using such platforms is associated with the subsequent growth in narcissism.

The results of this study suggest that both occur but show that posting selfies can increase narcissism.

Therefore, according to this study, not only does excessive social media use increase narcissism in certain situations, but posting selfies can increase narcissism as well. These are all things influencers must do to stay relevant.

According to the article "Narcissism and Fame: A Complex Network Model for the Adaptive Interaction of Digital Narcissism and Online Popularity":

Narcissists use social media excessively, to display their charismatic looks and, by their social skills, they can become social mavens or influencers (Moon et al. 2016). Instagram is an ideal platform for an individual to engage him/herself and to gain more visibility. This process of self-promotion involves the visual appearance of a person with a high number of followers who talk about his/her likability (Holtzman et al. 2010), and digital reputation is earned (Alshawaf and Wen 2015). They proactively gear themselves and their followers to increase the follower likability and engagement (Bernarte et al. 2015). An example of such behavior can be a selfie with lifestyle information (Alshawaf and Wen 2015), captioned by using hashtags (Page 2012). Often, they follow limited people and, thus, have a high follower to following ratio, indicating their high influence/popularity (Farwaha and Obhi 2019; Garcia et al. 2017).[47]

W. Keith Campbell wrote in his book with co-author Carolyn Crist, *The New Science of Narcissism: Understanding One of the Greatest Psychological Challenges of Our Time—and What You Can Do About It:*

Narcissists want a large audience, and they work hard for it. They search for others who will boost their status, request connections, and use social media platforms more often to get attention and status.

They thrive here because it's built around their environment—like lions thrive on the savanna and polar bears thrive in arctic habitats. . . . For narcissists (social media), it's also an avenue to fame and celebrity. Influencers with large followings are more likely to get noticed, draw in brand deals, and become famous. They don't necessarily need a publicist or agent if they're good enough at promoting themselves, so they work hard at it. This doesn't mean that promotion or fame are bad, simply that social media allows people to self-enhance, and self-enhancement is a key feature of narcissism.[48]

Does this mean all influencers are narcissists drawn to social media to live out all their wildest narcissistic fantasies? We cannot take an entire group of people and label them narcissists, especially if narcissism is characterized by a lack of empathy, entitlement, and exploitation, along with a need for attention. However, it does indicate that anyone attracted to a lifestyle that affords them fame and attention is probably more likely to possess narcissistic traits. Verity Jones, a former influencer and a freelance journalist, was self-aware enough to catch herself falling into a seductive, narcissistic, social media trap. She wrote an important opinion piece for *The Guardian* titled "I Was Insta-Famous and It Was One of the Worst Things to Happen in My 20s."[49] In the article, she says:

I became convinced that I was so fascinating. If I was the centre of attention on my phone, that should translate into being the centre of attention in real life. It makes you the worst kind of dick: entitled, self-obsessed, and *incredibly* dull because the only thing you think about is yourself.

Verity goes on to describe how being an influencer encouraged the worst parts of herself, including bringing out a narcissistic side of herself that she did not like:

Social media feeds those darkest parts of every personality, encouraging you to rant on Twitter, brag on Facebook, or be vain on Insta. Vanity sells on the 'Gram. The hotter the pic, the better it does, so the more time you spend in the mirror creating them. Staying Insta-famous relies on you mining the depths of your own narcissism.

The quote "Staying Insta-famous relies on you mining the depths of your own narcissism" is highly alarming, especially when looking at a study out of Britain, where one-fifth of children polled in the study are aspiring to be social media influencers or YouTubers when they become adults.

This study[50] polled two thousand British parents with at least one child between the ages of eleven and sixteen, and the top five aspirational professions chosen by the children were as follows: doctor (18 percent); social media influencer (17 percent); YouTuber (14 percent); veterinarian (13 percent); and teacher (9 percent). The top answers for why they wanted this job were as follows: for money (26 percent); for fame (22 percent); and because they know they would enjoy it (17 percent).[51]

Verity, the twenty-something ex-influencer we met above, is a clear example of how social media influencing can bring out a dark and narcissistic side in people, even if they were not narcissistic to begin with. Verity may be in the minority of people who can actually see what is happening to them and realize that is not the life she wants for herself. She recognized it was toxic and unhealthy and that she was part of a culture that makes people feel bad about themselves.

Verity's opinion piece peels away the beautiful filters of Instagram and gives us a real look at the ugliness beneath it. However, before further discussing the dark side of influencing, it is important to mention the good aspects of it. Some influencers help others feel less alone by sharing their vulnerable struggles and destigmatizing things such as mental illness, postpartum depression, and body image, to name only a few.

Activists, scientists and medical professionals who are influencing on social media can shed light on important causes and inspire people to act on important issues, especially related to injustice. Talented dancers, ice skaters, musicians, and creative types can bring joy, and comedians and humorous influencers bring laughs. Social media can be an excellent resource for businesses and is the perfect stage for them to display their work and gain new customers. There are many good reasons for people to grow a brand or business on social media. But just like anything else, there is also a dark side. One example of the darker parts of social media influencing is the lack of empathy, not only to others around the influencers but a blatant disrespect of others' cultures in certain instances.

*The Guardian* highlighted an example of this in Bali, where several influencers decided to stay during the coronavirus pandemic. Reports of careless behavior and other events that showed disrespect for the Balinese had continuously angered the public.[52] In the same article, Balinese politician and designer, Niluh Djelantik, asked the influencers who were staying in Bali to "have a little empathy," further stating, "The key for Bali recovery (from the pandemic) is the low number of (COVID-19) cases. But the foreigner who has (online) followers creates content about violating the health protocol, leaving an impression that Bali is not safe," Niluh said.

Because narcissism inflicts so much damage, it is no wonder that there are studies exploring the correlations between influencing and narcissism and what this means for an already growing epidemic of narcissism.

W. Keith Campbell and Jean Twenge started raising the alarm about the epidemic of narcissism when they published their book *The Narcissism Epidemic: Living in the Age of Entitlement* in 2009.[53] In the book, they draw upon their research of many years, describing their concern for the uptick of narcissism in American culture:

> Understanding the narcissism epidemic is important because its long-term consequences are destructive to society. American culture's focus on self-admiration has caused a flight from reality to the land of the grandiose fantasy. We have phony rich people (with interest-only mortgages and piles of debt), phony beauty (with plastic surgery and cosmetic procedures), phony athletes (with performance-enhancing drugs), phony celebrities (via reality TV and YouTube), phony genius students (with grade inflation), a phony national economy (with $11 trillion of government debt), phony feelings of being special among children (with parenting and education focused on self-esteem), and phony friends (with the social networking explosion).

When I asked W. Keith Campbell about how social media is contributing to a culture of narcissism through the influencer phenomenon, he told me:

> For normal people, the celebrity level of exposure is radical (through social media). A legit 1930s celebrity probably has had less exposure than a mediocre social media influencer today. When you are exposed to this, you get all sorts of celebrity problems: narcissism, body dysmorphia, eating disorders, competition, hyper self-focus on your appearance. The other thing, and this is more theoretical, is how people think about themselves. It used to be that people thought about themselves as moral agents (I want to be a good person versus a bad person), and then it changed more toward personality (I'm this kind

of a person: creative, nice, etc.). Then it changed to brands, where people had to become a brand, so to survive in a modern network social economy, you have to develop a brand. We've challenged young people to become brands with nothing, and that's incredibly hard because you have literally nothing to go on. When people do this, they either focus on looks or exotic locations, which is the influencer model, and then other paths you find food, or whatever—but usually you have to be physically attractive and go to exotic places. It's challenging for people to build your identity on getting likes for your looks—it's not a long-term strategy for success—it's a long-term strategy for misery.

If social media is our worst nightmare when it comes to the narcissism epidemic, then it is concerning how much it influences our lives. We have moved beyond reality television and YouTube and entered a world where TikTok stars are millionaires in their teens. If that becomes the aspirational standard for the younger generations around the world (as we are starting to see that it is), then we are encouraging and enabling a narcissistic lifestyle where the most important things in life are our image.

## NARCISSISTIC SNAKE OIL SALESPEOPLE ON SOCIAL MEDIA

The term "snake oil salesman" (essentially, a deceitful person exploiting others to make a profit from them) was first used in 1927 in the poem "John Brown's Body" by Stephen Vincent Benet. The goal of some influencers is to acquire enough of a following where they can start making a profit by selling products and doing advertisements. Often, they will offer a special discount code that followers can use to get a deal on whatever the influencer is promoting and selling.

While they are not selling literal snake oil, some influencers with large followings may prey upon innocent people and convince them they need something they do not with the purpose of lining the influencer's own pockets. Perhaps it is a cleanse or a supplement or a program that is guaranteed to deliver miraculous results. Sometimes, they promise wealth, prosperity, and that anyone can have the life they want—if they pony up a large amount of money. Some influencers can get very rich by exploiting others and promising them results that are unrealistic and unattainable.

How do we even know if the products influencers are selling us are any good or if they have used them personally? Even if they have tried the product, do they like it, or are they lying to us? It would be impossible to know who is truly genuine or if they are just trying to make money versus enhancing people's lives.

In December 2019, the BBC and an anonymous Irish presenter, "Blindboy," filmed three British influencers who agreed to promote a drink that contained hydrogen cyanide (a fatal chemical). Astonishingly, all three influencers agreed to endorse the drink without trying it first or checking the ingredients. They were told the fake weight-loss drink was named "Cyanora" and that the ingredients in the drink were magnesium, calamine, lemon balm, red clover, and hydrogen cyanide.

Once the influencers were told that hydrogen cyanide is poison and that they were set up, they were upset; clearly, they did not know hydrogen cyanide is literal poison. However, the point is that they were willing to promote something they knew nothing about and had not even tried for large sums of cash. (Apparently, one of the three influencers, Zara Holland, pushed back and said that her agent stated she would not promote a product without trying it first and that she needed more details before promoting it.)[54]

# MULTILEVEL MARKETING AND NARCISSISM ON SOCIAL MEDIA

In the early days of the COVID-19 pandemic, the Federal Trade Commission had to serve a stern warning to several multilevel marketing companies (MLMs) for making false claims that their products were solutions or cures to the virus. This practice was not only absurd, but dangerous, considering the best minds in science were still trying to unravel the mysteries of the novel virus. Perhaps even more insidious was that some of these influencers were trying to convince others to sell products "underneath" them, with the promise of total career autonomy and a glamorous lifestyle to boot. They were feeding off desperation—both that of people frightened of the virus, desperate for a cure and those who were in dire financial straits. Beyond this, hoping for career success via an MLM is a mirage. According to *The Daily Beast,* a 2017 Consumer Awareness Institute analysis of 350 MLMs alleged that 99 percent of participants lost money.[55]

The appeal of this model of marketing and sales is understandable. The way many of these companies draw people in is by promising the potential for a generous income, leading to a fabulous, financially worry-free lifestyle with luxury cars, dream homes, lavish vacations, and flexibility. If someone can make this lifestyle happen and be successful at it, then more power to them. If they totally believe in the product they are selling and want to share it with others, great.

But if 99 percent of people involved in MLMs lose money, it stands to reason that only 1 percent of people who participate will make money. To reach the top of the pyramid, one must recruit others to sell products underneath them. The more salespeople underneath them, the more profit they accrue. If there was blunt honesty about the actual success rates of this business model, the appeal would not be as strong to join in on the venture, and that's where the exploitation piece enters the picture.

Some of the few who may profit from MLMs may have narcissistic traits and knowingly exploit others by selling them a lifestyle that they will not ever be able to reach or sustain. Knowing that unsuspecting people will lose money at your gain requires a level of detachment. Detachment often goes hand-in-hand with a lack of empathy. In this business model, 95 percent of people quit within ten years, further highlighting that for most, it is unsustainable, even in the long run with persistence and perseverance.[56]

The first time I was recruited to join one of these businesses, I felt a warning go off in my gut. Someone I barely knew sent me a virtual chat message that felt a little overenthusiastic. I remember thinking, *What does she want from me?* She had never sent me a chat before, so I did not think it was to find out how I had been doing after all these years.

Sure enough, after asking me multiple questions about myself, as if we were long-lost best friends, she launched into a platform speech about joining her in her new business venture, trying to sell me on how amazing her life was and how burned out she used to be working in corporate America. If I joined the business with her, I, too, would be promised a level of success that I could only dream of without having to work too hard for it. I was too busy at the time to even entertain the idea, and I had already learned the hard way that a healthy dose of skepticism in life is generally a good thing. If something sounds too good to be true, it usually is.

In *Marie Claire,* Dr. Maire O'Sullivan, a lecturer in advertising and marketing at Edge Hill University in the United Kingdom, compared this type of interaction and recruitment to what is known as narcissistic "love bombing," saying:

Some of these companies have an alarmingly cult-like mentality, they practice "love bombing," and encourage you to cut off anyone who isn't supportive of the MLM or has concerns about the business model. That is alarming and abusive behavior.

Love bombing is common with narcissistic abuse and every narcissist, whether grandiose or vulnerable, uses it as tactic to manipulate and win people over to work into their agenda. Love bombing can consist of over-the-top behaviors and gestures that make you feel like you are living out a romantic comedy—except the ending is never a happy one. It is a type of predatory behavior that is part of the narcissistic profile. Love bombing is normally used in reference to romantic relationships, but anyone can be "love bombed" in any context—an overenthusiastic, over-the-top performance of false flattery, designed to lure someone in to fill a need for the narcissist.

One woman I interviewed for this book told me she feels like "Everyone is someone to get something from," when she has been approached by people asking her to join them as a downline in their MLM business. Others I know who have dabbled as salespeople in MLMs have told me they eventually felt guilt about trying to push things on their friends and stopped before they ruined some of their relationships.

It's concerning to think these business models that rely heavily on social media to recruit and sell products could encourage narcissistic and predatory behavior. As people lose money or struggle to get money back that they lost with MLMs, they might become more desperate to make it work, alienating family and friends in the process.

Most people who participate in or dabble with MLMs are victims of predatory practices. Then there are the few who are ruthless and don't care who they step on or exploit to get what they want. It is important to understand how certain people with narcissistic tendencies can exploit our good faith, especially when we are in a vulnerable place, because much of exploitation happens when we are feeling weak or not in the best place in life. Narcissistic types have a radar for identifying and exploiting vulnerable people. Maybe you are a new and sleep-deprived mom, or someone who recently lost a job, or perhaps someone who is just lonely and looking for community and friendship.

A woman named Angela who joined an MLM selling Tupperware spoke to the Huffington Post[57] about her experience and said that it felt like she had a new group of best friends who were, at first, constantly checking on her until it started getting pushy, with her new friends aggressively asking her to recruit more people under her. Angela had enough when her mother was diagnosed with advanced cancer and her colleagues told her she needed to use her mother's diagnosis to increase sales. "You need to use your mom's cancer as your sales pitch," they told her. "You need to turn it into a party and ask everyone that cares about you and your mom to help you sell Tupperware."

Angela left her MLM shortly after, explaining that things weren't what they seemed on the surface: "On paper, it looked like I made a lot of money. But I lost a lot of money," Angela said. "Every month, they would have a sales catalog and you had to buy samples to show at the parties. You also had kits that were always changing. So, whenever a product would change, you'd have to buy more so you could have it at the party."

Angela's story touches on the ugliest parts of narcissism on social media. She was expected to exploit her mother's serious diagnosis and take advantage of other people's empathy to sell Tupperware. Her team—people who were supposed to be her friends and rooting for her success—acted entitled to the point where they callously expected her to use a cancer diagnosis of a loved one to promote products. These requests were seriously lacking in empathy with the assumption that it was ever okay to ask Angela to do something like that.

Narcissism related to MLMs is fueled by social media because this is now where all the advertising, promoting, and recruiting is done. Just like everything else on social media, the best parts are highlighted, often exaggerated, or completely phony. It is critical that we learn how to protect ourselves from these predatory and exploitative practices on social media. The way we can protect ourselves and those we care about is to have knowledge about how these exploitative processes work and to know all the facts before jumping into a situation that could wreak havoc on our lives.

## NARCISSISTIC GURUS AND HEALERS ON SOCIAL MEDIA

There is growing interest in the mental health field in the narcissistic and predatory practices of some people in the healing spaces, motivational leaders, and wellness gurus. Social media has given these people a platform to take advantage of vulnerable people and simultaneously feed themselves with narcissistic supply.

Linda Martinez-Lewi, PhD, describes these particular people in the healing spaces as covert narcissists, charging exorbitant and unwarranted fees to people with the idea of luring them to continue to overpay through exploitation:

These human-embodied snakes take directly from the ideas of others, attractively package them, and use the force and magnetism of their personalities to sell these goods. They offer a shortcut to reaching a higher consciousness over weekends often named "intensives." The price tag on these "holy retreats" can cost in the thousands, easily. I have known a number of individuals who have gotten into these unfortunate situations with phony yogis who are narcissists and even socialized sociopaths.[58]

Often, a narcissistic healer will promise miracles or guaranteed healing from traumas or earlier wounding. None of us can promise complete healing to another person, and it is narcissistic to think that one person can be the sole reason for someone else's healing journey. An individual in the helping profession is supposed to be a guide and a support system, not a miracle healer.

Shahida Arabi, bestselling author and expert on narcissistic abuse, believes some of these covert, narcissistic healers knowingly prey on people who are survivors of previous narcissistic abuse, saying: "While there are many incredible therapists, coaches, spiritual guides, authors, bloggers and advocates in a number of different fields who can provide a great deal of rich wisdom to the survivor community, there are also predators who mask themselves as healers in order to gain narcissistic supply (praise, admiration and/or resources)."[59]

## Hayla's Story—Exposing the Toxic Side of the Wellness Industry Through Satire

Hayla Wong is currently a stay-at-home mom with a popular satirical Instagram account (@haylawong), described as "disrupting, writing about, and parodying BS in Spiritual Wellness." Hayla's account often features a parody character she refers to as "WooAnon Goddess." Hayla's account is sharp, witty, and takes aim at some of the problematic and/or narcissistic tendencies that can sometimes pop up in the wellness/healer spaces online.

Hayla started her journey to satirical criticism when she was using her Instagram account to market self-help services after taking about six months to gather several alternative wellness certifications—like Reiki and yoga. Hayla clarifies to me that yoga is not alternative and has cultural roots, but she tells me, "I approached it from a whitewashed and aesthetic perspective." Shortly after, she realized she could gain clients using social media: "I was getting some clients that I attracted using soulful/ sexy Insta captions mixed with New Age philosophical concepts, then the pandemic hit, and I got pregnant. I was also involved in a pyramid-like scam that presented itself as 'transcended feminist economy/community' at the time. Everything kind of came to a pause but I was still consuming a lot of online content of the esoteric/New Age type and was in virtual community with a lot of people of the same mindset, which is when I started seeing all the conspiracy theories and pandemic denial, and the love- and-light dismissal of racism."

Hayla has a formal education in sociology, and that helped inform her path to stepping back and digging deep. She tells me, "I snapped out of my New Age haze, which I got into post-abusive marriage and divorce . . . It took me about a year to fully reconcile my relationship with New Age spiritual wellness before I created the WooAnon Goddess character, pretty much drawing 'divine inspiration' from all the garbage I'd seen that year. I try to make it clear that this satirical character is what I could have genuinely become if I had kept going down that pipeline of influence. I also think it is my respon- sibility when I use satire to have nuanced discussions about the themes I introduce, or at least clarify my stance, hence all the more serious stuff, and lengthy captions."

Hayla's experience with the wellness industry has been strictly through social media and describes how she initially became attracted to the wellness culture on Instagram: "I first got attracted by mental health content which then spun me further out toward the fringes, which is also where some of the more toxic/dangerous content lives. For me, it was mental health—yoga—manifestation—mindset hacking—tantra (the whole divine feminine/masculine cis-het crap I talk about in many posts) and that's pretty much where I stopped."

After Hayla's experiences, she believes some wellness influencers are problematic and cause harm. Elaborating on this, she says: "I think they become harmful to their followers when they lack accountability, spread misinformation, lack intersectional understanding, weaponize their influence, and act beyond their scope of knowledge. I see many influencers create parasocial relationships and a false sense of community with their followers then use that relationship to manipulate them, using the typical tactics of control. What really concerns me the most is how many of the wellness influencers will frame their content/messaging as a form of healing or justice, while actually causing further harm. For example, recently I've been going after the divine gender trend that is really just repackaged cis-hetero sexism.

When I asked Hayla if she saw any connections with the problematic wellness influencers and narcissism, she told me the short answer is yes, but the long answer is more complex: "In an environment and industry where self is a commodity that you get to present and profit from as you see fit, a narcissist will probably do quite well." She continues by telling me a trend that's been bothering her among some of the New Age wellness coaches who use a concept called "triggering" as one of their healing modalities. Hayla says, "I find this incredibly problematic since most of these people are not trauma-informed or licensed psychotherapists, and they could further harm their client."

## SPOTTING A NARCISSISTIC INFLUENCER ON SOCIAL MEDIA: A THIN LINE BETWEEN HELPING AND EXPLOITING

I have personally suspected there are some covert narcissistic healers on social media. These people seem to get a high from feeling powerful, and nothing feels more exhilarating to a narcissistic guru than having others worship and fawn over them. Social media is where you will find not only a covert narcissist, but a communal narcissist, who is seeking to receive narcissistic supply from "helping" others. They do this while also exploiting their followers to pay them a lot of money for services they could find elsewhere—likely that are reasonably and appropriately priced and offered by a compassionate and well-trained professional. It's a communal narcissist's dream to receive praise and admiration for being an amazing and helpful person from an adoring audience, and social media is exactly where they will find that audience.

Narcissistic healers and gurus are not concerned with helping others; rather, they are interested in worship, attention, and money. Since social media provides them the ability to cast a wide net, they can cause more damage than they would otherwise. Anyone with a large following has a responsibility to act ethically and in the best interest of those who put their trust in them. These unethical people can also be so narcissistic and grandiose that they have convinced themselves that their path is the right one and that they are helping others by what they are doing. The greatest con of narcissism is actively harming people while thinking you are doing them a favor. When I spoke with W. Keith Campbell about the psychology of narcissistic healers and gurus, he told me:

> The spiritual system and the psychological system are somewhat separate, so you can have this narcissistic psyche, still be somewhat liberated, and you're channeling your enlightenment through your ego instead of your heart chakra.

Campbell also told me that narcissists and psychopaths enjoy meeting high-status people and taking photos with them, so you might have insight into a narcissistic influencer, guru, or healer by how many pictures of them you see in their social feeds that fit this description.

By adulthood, most of us know right from wrong, and while money, fame, followers, and positive attention can be enticing and validating, it is important to understand when we do things that could potentially exploit, mislead, or hurt other people. We should not let fantasies of power, adoration, and wealth corrupt our minds and hearts, especially if it involves stepping on others to get those things.

## CELEBRITY CULTURE AND NARCISSISM ON SOCIAL MEDIA

Narcissistic behavior was never more prominently displayed on social media than it was during the height of the lockdowns during the coronavirus pandemic, and some of the worst offenders were celebrities and tone-deaf wealthy people.

One study in the *Journal of Research and Personality*[60] found that celebrities are far more narcissistic than the general population and more than aspiring business leaders (MBA students) to whom they were both compared in the study. Interestingly, female celebrities were found to be more narcissistic than males, whereas there is more narcissism noted among males than females in the general population. In other not-so-surprising news of the study, reality stars were found to be the most narcissistic, followed by comedians, actors, and then musicians (out of all professions).

Finally, another interesting finding in that study was that it appears that celebrities may already have narcissistic tendencies when they enter the industry, so perhaps people with narcissistic tendencies are drawn to attention, fame, and seeking out celebrity status, even before it happens for them. The ruthlessness that narcissists possess is also what makes it easy for them to step all over others to get to the top.

During the pandemic, while people were losing their lives, jobs, stability, and security, some celebrities were obliviously posting photos on social media from their gorgeous homes, completely ignorant to the idea that the USA would ultimately end up in the worst recession since the Great Depression.[61] Many social media observers were annoyed, and even infuriated, when they not only saw celebrities lamenting about being quarantined, poolside from their mansions, but also baffled by how out of touch they seemed, going to parties and traveling when the average American was trying to just make it through the day while also preventing the spread of the virus.

An article in *The Atlantic* by Spencer Kornhaber described this justified anger. He depicted some of the backlash the Kardashians faced from their social media audience after flying dozens of friends to a private island to celebrate Kim's fortieth birthday in October 2020:

> The public quickly went into rage-LOL mode. Social-media users paired Kardashian's photo captions with images of cursed paradises: the Fyre Festival, a *Game of Thrones* wedding hall, a *Midsommar* ceremony, Hieronymus Bosch's *Garden of Earthly Delights*. Other responses to Kardashian's vacation pics simply expressed white-hot offense. One tweet with 4,300 likes: "You know what would have felt normal for me, Kim? Not having to say goodbye to my mother over FaceTime as she was dying of COVID . . . Rubbing this in our faces is cruel & clueless." Another tweet (from the rocker Peter Frampton, who has surely done some reckless partying in his time): "Are you that insensitive you don't realise this is not what the majority of people during the worst covid spike yet want to hear? People are going to food banks not private islands.[62]

A fair number of celebrities are entitled and believe rules do not apply to them, which is one of the most obnoxious aspects of a narcissistic celebrity. They believe they are above everything, usually because not many people say no to them once they reach a certain level of fame.

I once spoke to a gentleman who had worked security for A-list celebrities, and he told me he believed some of them were incredibly narcissistic and emboldened because they never heard the word *no* from anyone. Ironically, he added that they also became very paranoid and distrustful because when no one ever tells you *no,* and users are always trying to leech off of your fame and wealth, it becomes hard to trust anyone, which is a very sad way to live.

Certain celebrities are accustomed to a life of special treatment and can become entitled (if they were not already to begin with). They believe they deserve special treatment at all times and can fly into a rage when they don't receive it. Their reality is so obscured that they often cannot see how entitled and tone-deaf they can be, resulting in an army of people calling them out on their social media pages.

There was huge backlash when actress Gal Gadot and other celebrities filmed an Instagram video to the Beatles' song "Imagine" at the beginning of the coronavirus pandemic. Jon Caramanica addressed this in the *New York Times,* saying:

> On social media, Gadot and her crew were lambasted for bumblingly contributing, well, whatever this is as opposed to money or resources. Their genial naïveté is blinding them to the grossest sin here: the smug self-satisfaction, the hubris of the alleged good deed. The presumption that an empty and profoundly awkward gesture from a passel of celebrities has any meaning whatsoever borders on delusion—what you see in this video is nothing more than perspective-fogged stars singing into a mirror.[63]

Most people didn't have access to the true view of celebrity entitlement and lack of empathy for others' experiences before social media. Now, we see them in full display, unfiltered. With a simple click of a "share" button, a celebrity can give you a glimpse into their life, and more importantly their thought process.

Whether the celebrity is a true narcissist or simply out of touch and misguided, narcissistic behavior is damaging to everyone who follows these people. The unattainable standard of beauty they present—whether it is from a filter, Photoshop, plastic surgery, or the oodles of money they can spend on personal trainers, nutritionists, and personal chefs—sets an unrealistic expectation for what the norms should be. Then we buy their weight-loss supplements, or fat-burning teas, and hope we can look like them when, in actuality, they are doing so much more behind the scenes than popping a weight-loss pill.

As with many of the case studies we've been examining, what glitters isn't always gold behind the scenes. Celebrity life on Instagram and other social networking websites continuously sends an unhealthy message that we could all be happier if we were flying on private jets, buying Hermès bags, dining out at the best restaurants, hanging out with fun and important people at exclusive parties, and looking like cover models. However, aspiring to this is ultimately bad for our collective mental health. In fact, celebrities are not happier than the average person. They suffer from depression, anxiety, PTSD, low self-esteem, body image issues, substance abuse, and even suicide. No matter how much someone acquires, it will never be enough to make someone feel fulfilled or content if they are focused on the wrong things, like fame.

A study in the *Journal of Clinical Psychiatry* found that after extensive media coverage of a celebrity suicide, 23.4 percent of participants had attempted suicide following that media coverage.[64] Some ideas as to why this might happen could be due to the normalization of suicide through the media or a possible identification with the deceased. Considering we have access to an abundance of news and connection to celebrities through social media, this could potentially have implications on suicide risk following a celebrity suicide, which gives further importance to understanding how media may report on suicide in a way that is more responsible.

The narcissistic, materialistic, consumer-driven aspects of social media can negatively skew our perspective on life. The cliché "money can't buy you happiness" is true. If your basic survival needs are met, and you can live relatively comfortably to the point where you don't have anxiety about paying your bills or affording healthcare, then happiness is at about the same levels for all people. Money and fame do not save you from the human condition; terrible things can happen to anyone. Mental and physical illness can strike anyone, and if you don't have positive relationships or a good support system, then all the money in the world cannot help.

Influencer and celebrity culture give us a false promise of happiness and can leave us feeling empty after consuming too much of it. It is time to move away from selling people false hopes and dreams and giving them an unattainable standard to aspire to that will not necessarily fulfill them. We can reclaim our power from some of this toxicity by not allowing social media to influence us away from our authentic selves and what brings us individual happiness because happiness means different things to different people. When we think there is only one way to happiness and we are influenced by the narrative that tells us materialism, attention, and even physical perfection will bring us life satisfaction, we will only get further away from understanding what we need to live a rewarding life. By unplugging and staying away from social media and reminding ourselves that nothing that we are being sold, literally or figuratively, is going to truly fulfill us, we can focus on what truly matters to us.

# TIPS, TAKEAWAYS, AND FOOD FOR THOUGHT

1. What is your personal definition of success?
2. Write about what a meaningful, successful life looks like for you. Avoid writing about anything that requires admiration, monetary success, or fame. What are the things that make you feel a sense of happiness or contentment? You don't have to have those things in your life now and it could be something from your past. Think about smaller things like a great conversation with a close friend, a purring cat, or snuggling with your dog. Understanding what brings us feelings of peace and contentment are clues that we may want to cultivate more of those things or experiences in our life.
3. Think of a time when you viewed a post of a celebrity or influencer and it made you feel bad about yourself, or even annoyed. If you felt this way about any influencer or celebrity you follow, consider unfollowing the ones that even give you the tiniest feeling of annoyance or inadequacy. Cultivate a list of people to follow that uplift and inspire you.

# Chapter 5

# RELATIONSHIP RUPTURES: HOW NARCISSISM ON SOCIAL MEDIA HARMS RELATIONSHIPS AND HOW TO SPOT NARCISSISTIC PREDATORS

Relationships are complicated to begin with but throw social media into the mix and the potential minefields are abundant. From family feuds that start from Facebook posts, to friendships ruined due to seeing a different side of a friend online, to predatorial types lurking on dating apps, to intentionally seeking out affair partners on social media, the relationship ruptures and pain that they cause can be more common than we realize. At the root of many of these ruptures are narcissism and narcissistic tendencies of people who use these networking apps and websites to fill their narcissistic supply and selfish needs. While some relational ruptures because of social media are unintentional or are simply misunderstandings, we can still look at the why and how we use it that contributes to the breakdown of many of our most significant and important relationships.

## NARCISSISTIC FRIENDS ON SOCIAL MEDIA

The narcissistic behavior on social media we may observe from some of our friends can be at best amusing and at worst friendship ending. As I wrote this book and talked to many different people about their experiences of having a relationship change because of social media, it was confirmed for me that social networking is having an impact on our friendships, and more than we realize. For example, I spoke to someone who can barely tolerate a woman she used to call a best friend because of her over-the-top dances on TikTok and reels on Instagram.

Vivian, who I interviewed for this book, told me she delayed having children because she was scared at how hard parenthood would be based on the posts and blogs she saw from a few of her friends about parenthood. She told me that often they would feature photos of their children having tantrums and that the experience of parenthood seemed only grueling, with no moments of joy. She also felt uncomfortable and dismayed at the very personal details that were given about the children. She believed that it was a horrible violation of their privacy and felt that if her mother had shared those details or photos about her without her consent, she would have been humiliated, shamed, and horrified.

Of course, it's a disservice and inaccurate to portray parenting as only sunshine and roses, and normalizing the difficult aspects of being a parent is helpful and important. For Vivian, it was the oversharing that was most bothersome. Years after seeing these posts in her feed almost daily, she realized she kept delaying having a child because of someone else's oversharing, which often felt self-absorbed and narcissistic. Subconsciously, what she was exposed to on social media impacted a major life decision for her.

Others I spoke to for this book shared their experiences being close friends with aspiring or established influencers. The common theme they shared was feeling that their privacy was violated by being filmed all the time when they were together. They also felt they were not able to share any genuine experiences with their friend because they were always taking photos or videos of everything and constantly on their phones.

It is also important to note that some online behaviors that may seem narcissistic in nature or at the very least slightly annoying are not coming from narcissists but rather from well-meaning individuals. Understanding some of the underlying motivations for using social media, such as feelings of acceptance, validation, and belonging, are helpful in reminding us to extend some compassion to others (and even ourselves) instead of rolling our eyes.

## Brittany: Badass Feminist in Name Only

When Tammy first met Brittany, they clicked right away. They had plenty of things in common and were at the same stage of life as busy working mothers. Brittany was a successful entrepreneur with her own social media strategy business, and the two women quickly went from an occasional coffee to spending frequent time together on weekends, and eventually they became friends on social media too.

At first, Tammy didn't pay much attention to anything Brittany posted online, but as time went on, she started getting annoyed by what she saw. Brittany reveled in proclaiming on Facebook that she was a "badass feminist," which Tammy had no problem with. It was the constant repetition that bothered her. It felt like Brittany was hitting everyone over the head with her messages.

Tammy is all for women supporting women, and she especially loves seeing her friends do well and succeed, but there was something about the way Brittany posted that felt disingenuous, even narcissistic, to her. The tone was completely different from the posts that her other friends were sharing. Brittany loved to show off and thrived off the attention she got. She made sure everyone knew she had the best, handsomest, and most-involved husband. She had the best job—and was the best at doing it—was fit and worked out religiously, was an attentive and involved mother, and loved to brag about how she could do it all, knowing that many of her friends were struggling trying to juggle everything.

Tammy started seeing a whole new side of Brittany, one that she had not seen in person, before they connected on social media. *Who is this woman?* Tammy thought to herself as Brittany's posts began to feel increasingly grandiose.

Tammy felt the best way to keep the friendship intact was to just mute and hide Brittany's posts. Even after she did that, she started to find some of Brittany's comments through text and in-person conversations taking the same haughty, disinterested tone. Brittany was judgmental and frequently looked down on others. She often gossiped about her friends to Tammy behind their backs, texting constant complaints and haughty statements like "I'm so tired of Jenny always complaining about her love life when she keeps making the worst decisions in men. Doesn't she realize I have a business to run and children to raise? I don't have time to hear about this bullshit!" During the pandemic she would also text things to Tammy that were critical, indifferent, and uncaring: "All the people dying are obese or lazy. I'm in such great shape that I don't have to worry about getting seriously ill from this virus."

Brittany also prided herself on making all the "right" decisions and was impatient with those in her life that she felt were doing the "wrong" things. She'd text things like, "Sandy is dating another loser. His clothes look like he got them from Goodwill," and "Bridgette had an okay wedding, but it was nothing like mine," or, "If Lola wants to move up the career ladder, she could use a few pointers from me. She's never going anywhere." No one was as good as she was.

Tammy eventually had enough of Brittany's callous, detached comments and the grandiose glorification of herself on social media. She observed that Brittany's actions often contradicted many of the things she posted about online. For example, Brittany prided herself on being an intersectional feminist and owned her own business. Her social media posts were of her at the Women's March or talking about women's rights in the workplace. She especially thought of herself as an advocate for working mothers, using her social media accounts to share articles and musings about the topic. While she often talked about women's rights and lifting other women, in real life Brittany underpaid her female employees and exploited her female interns by making them work for free even though she could afford a stipend. She also caused major financial headaches for her consultants by overworking them and stalling their checks to the point they considered taking her to collections.

Tammy and Brittany are no longer friends. The rupture between Tammy and Brittany shows how social media can highlight narcissistic traits in people that otherwise may not be as obvious in person, at least at first. Would Tammy still be friends with Brittany today had they never become social media friends? It's hard to say. Tammy really liked Brittany until she saw a different side to her on social media, but as she got to know her better and spent more time with her, she also noticed narcissistic traits in conversations and that her proclamations of being a feminist were directly contradicted by how she treated the female employees she claimed to champion.

Tammy noted that Brittany was always much more pleasant in person. While she believes Brittany is narcissistic, she admits that her personality on social media was where her narcissistic traits were on full display for all to see. It was like she could not help herself.

It is possible that Brittany is just insecure and uses social media for validation and to cover self-doubt. However, Brittany's social media narcissism and some of her general narcissistic and exploitive behaviors highlight how those narcissistic features displayed online can interfere with and disrupt friendships.

## NARCISSISM AND THE ANNOYING POSTS THAT DRIVE OUR FRIENDS BONKERS

While many people who are not narcissists can annoy their friends and loved ones on social media, these platforms offer a unique way to spot red flags with the people in our lives who have narcissistic traits and don't contribute to our well-being. These online warning signs may also indicate we are not only dealing with a narcissist on social media, but also in real life.

Beyond these things, I was curious to find out what types of posting the average person found annoying, self-centered, or narcissistic. Anecdotally, I know many people who are annoyed or put off by certain types of posts and plenty of folks who take advantage of the "mute" button (a way to hide people's posts without having to "unfriend" them). It seems that almost anyone you talk to who uses social media has had some type of irritation with a friend or family member because of it.

There are countless articles circulating about the most annoying social media posters, but here are the most frequently mentioned that relate to social media narcissism:

**Selfies.** People are universally annoyed by selfies posted in excess. Research confirms that posting a lot of selfies correlates with narcissism. Again, it does not mean that *everyone* who posts selfies, or even excessively so, is a narcissist, but there is a connection, and this type of posting is what many people associate with social media narcissism.

**Excessive public displays of affection and bragging about your amazing life.** Nobody likes a bragger who constantly shares about their fantastic life. Most people are also turned off by over-the-top displays of affection that some couples post (especially if it is a post that is dedicated to someone who isn't on social media. For example: "Happy Birthday to the best husband in the world, even though he is not on Facebook and will never see this post!" Obviously, why do this if the object of your affection will not see it?

The over-the-top braggers are not necessarily narcissistic, but there is a correlation between narcissism and excessive posting. The "bragging about my fantastic life" posts are often attention seeking and in search of validation. This could be a sign of a narcissistic person, but it could also be someone who is insecure and wants attention, or for other reasons.

**"Vague booking."** This is essentially what it sounds like: people posting status updates that say something cryptic that is impossible to know what it is really about. For example, "Something really bad happened today and I am so upset."

A vague status update could also be about another person and used as a passive-aggressive way to express a frustration with them. For example, "Some people are really hitting my last nerve today."

Adolescents on social media may do the vague booking thing more often because they have not necessarily learned how to identify and express their emotions properly.

This could also be a feature of a grandiose or vulnerable narcissist, although more likely a vulnerable one since they are much more likely to be passive-aggressive and silently angry. However, grandiose narcissists can be passive-aggressive as well, and they may use tactics like vague booking to confuse and to make their targets feel bad.

Alternatively, vague booking can just be innocent attention seeking. The person doing it may not even realize the motivation behind it is simply wanting attention. It may also be a cry for help for someone who could be deeply depressed and unable to express themselves properly. In these situations, we should exercise our compassion.

**Humblebragging.** The humblebrag (a brag sprinkled with a dose of humility) and its annoyance factor has some legitimate research behind it. Most humblebragging is done on social media because it's the easiest place to share thoughts and receive instant gratification in the form of praise. For example, "Lost power at the vacation house today! So annoying!" In this post, the person is highlighting the fact that they have a vacation house while throwing in a woe-is-me statement, so it is not as blatantly offensive as "Hey everyone! Look at my awesome vacation house!"

A 2018 research study published in *the Journal of Personality and Social Psychology* found that people actually like you less if you humblebrag as opposed to straight-up bragging.[65]

*Time Magazine* wrote an article on this study, sharing from it that:

> Out of 646 people surveyed, 70 percent could recall a humblebrag they'd heard recently. Next, they established that there are two distinct types of humblebrags. The first falls back on a complaint ("I hate that I look so young; even a nineteen-year-old hit on me!") while the second relies on humility ("Why do I always get asked to work on the most important assignment?"). About 60 percent of the humblebrags people remembered fell into the complaint category. [66]

The reason "regular bragging" is seen as more palatable is because it comes across as more sincere, and people generally respond positively to sincerity. The researcher conducting this study, Ovul Sezer, quoted in the *Time* article, says to try to go easy on humblebraggers, as we may be doing it, too, without realizing it. That's the thing about humblebragging—it is easier to do than to straight-up brag because it doesn't sound outwardly grandiose—something most of us have been conditioned to avoid.

We've established that it's annoying, but is humblebragging on social media a sign of narcissism? Done in excess, it certainly could be, but we need to examine the context. Humblebragging might be more common because people (especially women) are taught from a young age not to celebrate our successes. We are told humility is a good thing, and of course it is! It's an opposing trait of narcissism, but too much humility is not necessarily what we should strive for. Everything in moderation!

It is important for us to distinguish what is truly narcissistic and what might actually be shame or trauma. If we are told from a young age to not celebrate ourselves and our joys, which we rightfully should be able to do, then we become adults who think showing any kind of pride in the self is wrong. We should all be able to share our joy and success genuinely and without fear of being judged or shamed.

For women—who have from the beginning of time stifled our accomplishments, goals, joys, and successes—it is especially important that we should be able to proudly claim them, on social media or otherwise. If someone else is angry or threatened by your success, that is on them, *not you.*

That said, it is always tricky to figure out the balance. How much bragging is too much? What sounds obnoxious? How do I share something proudly without coming across as narcissistic? Because most of us care about what others think—at least to a degree—many of us are self-conscious about these things.

At the end of the day, it is more about who we share things with. Those closest to us, who truly care deeply for us, want to hear about our joys and share our happiness. For those of us who are more of the self-conscious types, perhaps smaller social media accounts, like a group with trusted friends and family as followers, is a solution for wanting to feel authentic on social media. Doing this ensures—hopefully—that your followers feel genuinely happy for you when things are up and genuinely sad for you when things are not going your way.

**Mean ranting.** We've all known people who get on their virtual soapbox and rant—about politics, bad drivers, the media, etc. While annoying to most—especially if you don't share the same viewpoint—this, too, needs to be examined in context. Mean, offensive, unfiltered ranting seems more in line with someone who is narcissistic, specifically a grandiose type. Judgment, criticism, and cruelty are a big part of the profile of narcissistic people, and social media is another tool through which to inflict their misery. Generally, outwardly cruel behavior is a feature of narcissism, and people who say and do mean-spirited things without much remorse should be avoided at all costs anyway.

While there are probably many more types of posts that agitate people online, the ones listed above are the most common. Unsurprisingly, these are all related to narcissistic traits!

It is important to keep in mind that it's easy to unintentionally construct an obnoxious post that may irritate others. Again, it is important to search for the combined red flags of narcissism: excess, lack of empathy, entitlement, exploitative behaviors, and self-centeredness.

## RULES FOR BEING A GOOD SOCIAL MEDIA CITIZEN

How can we make sure our online behavior doesn't put us in a bad light to others? First, look inward, and before you start typing, ask yourself what your motivations are for posting. If it is because you want attention, where in your life are you not getting attention? Will social media validation fill that need?

Is it because someone has angered you? While posting your grievance is certainly easier than a face-to-face conversation, consider the long-term consequences of airing this dirty laundry online. It could be a simple misunderstanding, yet you might damage a relationship forever. If you're angry with someone, have the courage to pick up the phone and talk to them before you type.

If something good has happened to you—an accomplishment,

buying a new house, etc.—ask yourself why you need to post about it. Is it to make someone envious? If so, why?

# FAMILY DYNAMICS, NARCISSISM, AND SOCIAL MEDIA

## Laurie: Sibling Rivalry Gone Wrong

Danielle's sister Laurie is ten years older than her and had given her trouble for as long as she could remember. Danielle's childhood memories with Laurie were filled with torture, torment, and physical assault. While her parents intervened in the fights, Laurie continued, often accusing Danielle of lying about the abuse. Danielle still has flashbacks about these horrible events and shudders recalling the time Laurie threw her down a flight of stairs. Danielle is a gentle and sensitive soul and believed in the importance of family, so she continued a relationship with Laurie when they grew to adulthood, thinking maybe Laurie's actions were just sibling rivalry. Danielle soon realized that Laurie had deeply rooted issues that played out both in real life and on social media.

Danielle was not the only relationship Laurie had tried to destroy. She'd been married and divorced many times, her multiple husbands unable to deal with her need to be the absolute center of attention, no matter what. She'd undergone multiple rounds of cosmetic surgery and had changed her hairstyle seemingly with every season. Like the sun, everything had to revolve around her, and when it did not, she made sure it would.

On Facebook, Laurie would post a ludicrous number of selfies from her pool with her best friend, labeling them "Hot girls in a hot tub!" Danielle and her siblings would laughingly screenshot and forward the selfies, believing them to be the harmless side of Laurie's narcissism.

When Danielle's husband unexpectedly passed away, the family immediately rallied around her to console and provide comfort to Danielle during a devastating time in her life. That is, everyone but Laurie. Laurie became resentful of Danielle because with the death of her husband, the attention was now completely on her, and Laurie was in the background. Laurie was not shy about hiding these feelings and said to Danielle with an eye-roll, "Now that your husband is dead, you're the favorite daughter."

This selfish comment was the last straw for Danielle. She realized that Laurie was toxic and that she could never have a healthy relationship with her. She stopped speaking to Laurie and cut her out of her life altogether. This threw Laurie into a retaliatory fit of narcissistic rage, and she blocked the entire family on Facebook. This might not have bothered most of them, but she had other plans: she would use social media as a tool to create problems and stir up drama. After Laurie blocked Danielle and her other siblings on Facebook, she called her mother crying. "They all hate me and it's your fault. You always picked sides," she told her mother. "Now they don't want to have anything to do with me, they all blocked me on Facebook and won't answer when I call," she lied. Her mother was blindsided and confused but had some sort of blind spot when it came to Laurie. She was the one person in the family who could always be manipulated by Laurie.

Laurie continued her virtual assault by using Facebook to send passive-aggressive messages to her family through an unwitting mutual Facebook friend, Bonnie. For example, Laurie and Danielle's parents lived in California, where they grew up, and for holidays, Laurie would tell her parents she could not visit them for various reasons and would then go on a tagging spree with Bonnie, letting her family know that she was, in fact, local during the holidays and purposely not seeing her parents. Laurie's parents who were also Facebook friends with Bonnie would see Bonnie and Laurie together in the posts and would know that Laurie made no effort whatsoever to see them.

Danielle told me that Laurie's social media behavior always felt intentional and vindictive to her, and she could never understand the thought process behind lying to someone and then posting it all on social media to blatantly showcase those lies.

What Laurie did to her family are typical things a narcissistic person might do: use online posts to cause drama and get attention, while also using it to send messages that she knew would hurt others.

Family dynamics can be fraught, and social media has added a whole new layer to relationships that are often already tense to begin with. Lots of people fight with their family for all to see online over various opinions, usually political, and that in itself has created familial rupture that is way more intense than it would have been before social media existed.

When we do have continuous and difficult interactions with family members on social networking sites, it is important to know that we can put up boundaries with how we engage with them. As trying as it can be when we have to be firm and stand our ground with family, we often have to do it for the sake of our sanity. Some people feel it is best not to be friends with certain family members on any social media sites, and some block them completely. Others have even deactivated from all social media to free themselves of the drama that sometimes comes with family dealings online, and they have felt completely liberated doing so. Family relationships are very personal, and only you can decide what is best for you and how you communicate and engage with them on social media.

# ROMANTIC RELATIONSHIP RUPTURES AND NARCISSISM ON SOCIAL MEDIA

## Grace and Gary: Red Flag Warning

When Grace, a pretty, single thirty-two-year-old met Gary out at a bar one night on a business trip out of town, she did not think much of it when he found her and friended her on Facebook the next day. Although his Facebook profile revealed that he had friends, most of his posts—what few there existed—were pictures of him solo.

Grace and Gary were soon messaging constantly through Facebook. He was incredibly charming and flattering—he commented and liked all her pictures and showered her with compliments, telling her how beautiful she was. He made his intentions crystal clear: he felt lucky he had found a woman like Grace and wanted to pursue a long-distance relationship with her. Soon, Grace started receiving flowers and extravagant gifts from Gary, even a designer purse that was worth several thousand dollars. *How was I so lucky to find a man like this?* Grace thought.

It had been months since they saw each other in person after that first meeting at the bar, but Grace was falling hard for Gary. She had never known a man who was so invested in her and her happiness before. He put her on a pedestal and treated her like a goddess—what more could she want?

Eventually, Gary was able to visit her on a weekend trip, and the two days and nights they had together exceeded all her romantic expectations. He even talked about engagement, marriage, and having kids. Grace was crazy about her nieces and nephews and had always wanted to be a mother. She thought, *For the first time in my life, everything is falling into place. My dreams of a man to love me forever are coming true.*

There was one peculiar incident during that weekend, but Grace was so intoxicated by the intense feelings of romance that she shrugged it off. Grace and Gary had taken a selfie together out at a restaurant, and Grace had posted it on her Facebook page, tagging Gary in it. With all the talk about the future, Grace was excited to share her status as "in a relationship" and to introduce her new beau online to all her friends.

Gary got the notification about the post and immediately freaked out, yelling, "What were you thinking tagging me in that picture? Take it down—now!" Grace was taken aback by his sudden outburst of anger and quickly deleted it. When Gary calmed down, he apologized profusely and explained to her that he was nervous because he was a very private person and had security clearance with his job as a government contractor that could get him in trouble at work.

It didn't occur to Grace that this didn't make sense, since Gary had an online presence in the first place. She didn't look too deeply into it and bought the explanation. She just wanted to move on from the incident and start planning their future together. Her bubble would burst shortly after Gary returned home.

Grace's phone rang in the middle of the night, waking her up. "This is Sue, Gary's wife," said the caller. "I'm sure he didn't tell you about me, or about our three children."

"What? No, that's not possible," said Grace.

"Believe it. You aren't the first time he's cheated. He usually meets women online and tries to keep it secret, but I always find out."

Horrified, Grace had a sleepless night and confronted Gary the next day. Without missing a beat, he said, "I'm so sorry, babe. We've been separated for a while. She just can't read the writing on the wall. She'll say and do anything, even lie like this. Just block her number."

Grace felt the pit in her stomach grow as she started to piece together all the red flag warnings she had ignored. Gary was available only at certain times, most of it was through Facebook messenger, and their phone calls were at odd times of the day and sometimes quite brief. Gary told Grace that because of his job he had limited availability and that's why many of the phone calls were very quick, but Grace came to realize it was likely because his family was within earshot and he stepping away to call her.

Grace also realized that even if Gary was telling the truth and he and his wife were separated, he had never mentioned children. The fact that he left out such a major aspect of his life made her realize that he couldn't be trusted. If he lied about something like that, what else would he lie about later? Grace picked up the phone and called Gary to end things with him once and for all:

"Please do not call me again, I never want to hear from you again, and if you ever do attempt to contact me, I will block you, IMMEDIATELY."

"If you want to believe my ex, that's fine. I never would have pegged you for someone who would be so gullible and give up on a good thing so easily," he snapped nastily.

After that call, Grace also spoke with Gary's wife, Sue, one final time. "For the first time, I've finally started talking to some divorce lawyers. I've turned a blind eye to Gary's affairs over the years, not to mention all the emotional and physical abuse," Sue said with a heavy voice.

"I'm so sorry this happened to you, but I am grateful you told me and that I didn't progress this relationship any further," Grace told Sue.

As Grace hung up the phone, she breathed a sigh of relief realizing she had dodged a bullet. Nevertheless, she had been so emotionally invested that she would go on to have trust issues after this experience for years to come.

## NARCISSISM AND INFIDELITY ON SOCIAL MEDIA

Narcissistic predators like Gary have found that social media has offered countless ways for them to commit infidelity. Chat groups, social networking sites, and other apps easily let them satisfy their need for narcissistic supply from unwitting partners.

According to a General Social Survey (GSS) between 2010 and 2016, 20 percent of men and 13 percent of women reported having a sexual encounter or relationship outside of their marriage.[68] With the rise and popularity of social media, there have been more opportunities for people to be unfaithful and also to get caught for their indiscretions.

The current research suggests a correlation between infidelity and narcissism, psychopathy, and Machiavellianism (a personality trait that consists of manipulation, cunningness, and calculation to use whatever means necessary to gain power). These three traits are known as the "dark triad" because of their exceptional malevolence. All three of the traits of the dark triad have been individually linked to infidelity, but one study, using a large retrospective survey, "found that all three traits correlated with reporting an infidelity at some point in a current (or most recent) relationship."[69]

Another study from 2014, which assessed 123 couples, found that infidelity and narcissism were related and infidelity "was driven by all four facets of sexual narcissism—sexual exploitation, grandiose sense of sexual skill, sexual entitlement (Study 1 only), and lack of sexual empathy (husbands only)."[70]

When you throw social media into the mix with narcissistic people, infidelity is going to have more of an opportunity to emerge. In fact, numerous studies have been done showing that social media is contributing not only to a rise in infidelity, but to romantic disengagement as well.[71] Also, spending an excessive amount of time on Twitter has been linked to conflict between romantic partners, which could potentially lead to infidelity, breakup, or divorce.

Social networking sites are addicting and can connect you to many people to whom you would not otherwise be connected, and because of these vast number of connections and the ease of striking up a casual conversation online, an emotional (breaking boundaries of a committed relationship without becoming sexual) or physical affair could be easy to fall into. Narcissistic types are thrill seeking and get bored easily, and with their lack of empathy, social media is a place for them to get narcissistic supply. Others who are not very narcissistic may be feeling something lacking in their marriage or partnership and fall into an emotional affair online that could turn sexual.

A study looking at online infidelity and narcissism, extraversion, and gender found that narcissism is also a predictor of emotional infidelity online.[72]

The appeal of online infidelity was discussed in a study in the *Journal of Computer-Mediated Communication:*

> Among the personality factors that contribute to the development of a desire for an online affair, narcissism seems to play a pivotal role. Apart from its significant link to infidelity in "real life," narcissism has specific relevance to online communication. Seiden (2001)[73] describes the Internet love story as a narcissistic accelerator, which enables people with narcissistic tendencies to meet online and create a mutual tale that flatters their grandiosity.[74]

Social media is clearly a place where narcissistic people get their thrills as they are frequently bored and need stimulation. For many narcissists, writing text is the easiest way to express flattery and love bomb someone. Social media is a tool narcissistic types can use to really turn on the charm, using the written word to make someone fall head over heels for them. Always be aware of excessive fawning in the early stages of dating, especially if it is done online.

## RELATIONSHIP CONFLICTS BECAUSE OF DIGITAL NARCISSISM

Beyond offering more avenues for infidelity, there are other ways that social media can cause fissures in a romantic relationship. For example, jealousy, addiction, over-sharing something personal about a significant other, and comparison to others are things that can easily cause conflict.

True narcissists want to make their partners jealous, relishing in envisioning them anxious and distressed. Narcissistic online behavior as it relates to romantic relationships can range from being slightly problematic to, at its worst, emotionally abusive. On the milder side, someone who is more self-centered rather than cruel may not be thinking about how they make their partner feel when they post something that might make their partner uncomfortable. They simply seek immediate self-gratification but do not intend to upset their partner.

If someone posts online content about their partner that is deeply personal, airs dirty laundry about the relationship—or really anything that crosses a boundary—it signals they are not considering their partner's feelings. If someone expresses displeasure with any online postings, and the poster nevertheless continues, then there is intentional malice and disrespect happening. Blatant, willful, and intentional disregard for the boundaries and comfort of the other person is textbook narcissism.

An insecure person, not necessarily narcissistic, may use social media to make their partner jealous. They might equate jealousy to caring. A narcissist, however, is malevolent and uses jealousy as a way to torment the other person.

How can you know the difference between the two? A person who is not a narcissist will ultimately feel remorse if they do something that hurts their partner, while a narcissist will not and will continue to repeat the problematic behaviors. Narcissists are always pushing boundaries.

Facebook jealousy and surveillance (checking a romantic partner's Facebook page) were found to be positively associated with anxiety in one study.[75] For example, someone may observe their partner becoming Facebook friends with an attractive man or woman, or in another situation, the partner is still friends with an ex on the site. The observance of these events may inspire even more surveillance and checking, which leads to more jealousy and anxiety. Therefore, the more one observes these occurrences, the more jealous and anxious they feel. Facebook surveillance that is defined as cyberstalking will be explored later on in this book. While it is hard to say whether the person who became anxious due to surveillance of their partner's social media page was predisposed to anxiety or the anxiety was only created because of the surveillance on social media, jealousy stemming from social media certainly exacerbates anxiety no matter how you look at it.

Even very secure people sometimes get jealous and feel threatened in their relationships, and social media doesn't help. For example, if someone sees their partner following and liking the posts of Instagram models, especially if the photos are sexually explicit, it would be a normal reaction to feel annoyed or jealous. We all want to feel special in our relationships, and we want to believe we are the most attractive to our partners, even if we do not mind if they find other people attractive (which is completely normal and expected). The biggest underlying issue in any relationship conflict is whether your partner respects you and your boundaries and expresses concern if you are upset about something. A good partner should also have the willingness to change or modify behavior that is hurtful or harmful to you.

Selfies are also associated with lower-quality relationships, according to a study where the researchers suggest that "selfie-related conflicts" cause jealousy in relationships because of excessive individual photo-sharing and commenting on those photos from other people. Furthermore, by sharing favorable images, the person creates an ideal online persona in their mind that "diverges from real life and these conflicts in turn reduce perceived quality of the romantic relationships." The results from the study concluded that "jealousy and the online ideal persona have a negative effect on romantic relationship over time."[76]

If lots of selfies are related to narcissism, even if the act of taking selfies seems relatively harmless on the narcissism spectrum, it still has the potential to cause problems in relationships. If we don't want certain social media behaviors to erode our relationships, it's worth it to self-reflect on whether our social media behaviors are having a negative impact on them. If they are, where do we need to pause, self-reflect, and modify for the sake of our relationships?

Do we do things on social media that make our partners uncomfortable or put them in an awkward position? Do we post things on social media that make our partners feel shame or embarrassment?

Do we post things on social media that we know might make them jealous? Do we spend too much time on social media, and does that take away from our quality time with our partners? Does comparing ourselves to others make us resent our own relationships? While some of these things may seem relatively harmless, they have the potential to cause issues down the road. On the bright side, with awareness and an investment in the well-being of our relationships, all these things can be self-corrected before too much damage is done.

## CATFISHING AND NARCISSISM

## Fang and Charlie: Flattery and Fraud

Annie's mother, Fang, was sixty years old when she met Charlie on an app for adults looking for friends and companionship. Fang, a Chinese immigrant, had been through plenty of trauma in her lifetime. She was in an abusive marriage for many years before she divorced Annie's father and was desperately lonely. She had never dated before and had no idea how or where to find companionship, so an app was an easy and obvious choice for her.

When Fang started talking to Charlie on the app, she was excited to finally find someone who seemed like he genuinely wanted to get to know her. Charlie told Fang that he was American, in his forties, serving in the military, and currently stationed in Syria. He sent her a series of photos of a handsome, blond, blue-eyed man, and doted on her with flattering messages that soon turned romantic. In addition to the photos he would send, they also spoke on the phone once or twice. While Fang thought the voice did not seem to match the photos, she was too infatuated at the time to notice the red flags.

Charlie showered Fang with attention and praise, telling her how beautiful she was. "I long to kiss you, and to make love to you," he told her. Fang fell for the flattery. She believed she was in love with Charlie. Her marriage had been filled with abuse and disrespect, so she fell hard for Charlie, someone who seemed to adore her.

Before long, Charlie told Fang that he wanted to open his own business but that he didn't have the start-up funds. Fang was retired and had very little money, but because she was frugal and only spent money on necessities, she had some cash savings and a modest investment in a retirement account.

Charlie, totally unashamed, outright asked Fang for money, and soon after she was wiring him $2,000. He didn't stop there. He kept asking for more, always offering some excuse for why he needed it—and the amount he needed became larger with each request. Fang never hesitated, obediently following his instructions to deposit money in the same bank, sometimes to different accounts. In a period of three weeks, she made eleven deposits, ranging between $2,000 and $50,000, ultimately totaling over $93,000.

This cleaned out Fang's savings. She told Charlie she could not give him anymore because there was nothing left to give. It was at this point when Charlie turned on her and began threatening her, saying he was going to send the police after her. He made threats like this to her because he knew they would scare her and she would believe them, hoping he could coerce her into giving him more money.

Suffice to say, Fang was devastated and distraught. Not only had she drained her savings account, but the man she thought she loved was now aggressive and threatening. She called her daughter Annie hysterical, screaming and crying. When Annie realized her mother had given away nearly $100,000—all her money—to an online stranger, she felt an intense anger wash over her.

Fang was clearly the perfect victim for Charlie, and he had systematically groomed her. She was a survivor of decades of abuse, and while she had children, they were now adults living on their own and busy with their own jobs, families, and interests. Fang was so lonely that her judgment was impeded. Charlie took advantage of a woman with deep trauma, loneliness, and vulnerability. Unfortunately, there are narcissistic people in the world like Charlie who face few consequences, if any, for their malice.

Although the incident with Charlie happened years ago, Fang still lives with trauma symptoms, which are only exacerbated by her prior trauma from her abusive marriage. She is terrified, believing that Charlie is coming after her because he knew where she lived. Every time an unknown number—or even a call identified as spam—shows up on her phone, she becomes nervous and anxious, thinking it's Charlie. Her blood pressure has gone through the roof from the anxiety. She flinches every time there is a knock at the door and gets upset with Annie if she sends her any packages that do not fit in the mailbox, because someone must knock on the door to deliver it, and Fang believes that Charlie will one day be at the door to harm her.

Currently, thanks to financial help from her children, Fang is looking to live in a gated community so she can feel safer. Because she gave so much personal information to Charlie, and he threatened her numerous times, she remains convinced that it is just a matter of time before he finds her and harms her.

When Annie reflects on what happened years ago, she now sees how easily something like this could have happened to her mother. Her mother was not a tech-savvy person and didn't know how to navigate the Internet. She did not understand the perils of narcissistic and sociopathic people who are waiting to prey on vulnerable and lonely victims on social media.

Annie would like others reading this to know that talking to their elderly parents and making them aware of online scamming is a good place to start when it comes to awareness about narcissistic predators. In hindsight, she says she would have paid attention and asked deeper questions about her mother's life beyond just saying, "How's work?" Instead, "What have you been doing after work?" "Are you *meeting any new people?*"

What happened to Fang is called "catfishing" and is "a deceptive activity where a person creates a fictional persona or fake identity on a social networking service, usually targeting a specific victim. The practice may be used for financial gain, to compromise a victim in some way, to intentionally upset a victim, or for wish fulfillment."[77] Catfishing has become somewhat of an online phenomenon, and one of the personality traits behind those that engage in this is narcissism.

In a study exploring the personality traits of people who catfish, it was found that "perpetrators tended to be males who were narcissistic, and who disclosed little about their true selves to their catfish partner.

Moreover, the perpetrators' families of origin were characterized by abuse, mental illness, and affective disorders."[78]

People who catfish could also be sociopaths or psychopaths, who share similar traits to narcissists, such as low empathy and exploitation of others. Narcissists, psychopaths, and/or sociopaths (psychopathy and sociopathy are very similar) have little to no conscience and no real attachments to others. If a narcissist is severely disordered, they will be closer to a psychopathic personality with no empathy; others are only objects to them. Other people are only useful when they serve a purpose for these dark, dangerous personality types.

Some people who catfish are doing it because of their feelings of a lack of self-worth and insecurity, and narcissistic people can be insecure, especially in their subconscious. One research study interviewed people who identified as catfishers and found that 41 percent were doing it out of loneliness. Others were dissatisfied with their physical appearance, and some did it out of a desire to escape their lives.[79] While these are motivations for catfishing, they may or may not be coupled with a narcissistic personality type.

## Protecting Yourself from Catfishing

The most malicious and dangerous people who engage in catfishing are more likely to have narcissistic personality traits. It's important to learn about the potential warning signs first in order to protect yourself and your loved ones. Here are some helpful tips, and while a few may seem obvious, it's always good to remind ourselves of these things.

**Be suspicious of any stranger who tries to friend you on social networking websites.** It's likely that, at one point or another, you've received a friend request from a total stranger. Someone trying to catfish may be one of these people, especially if you don't have any common friends, interest groups, or causes. The motives behind these types of requests are usually suspect, so use your judgment. Most of the time, it is a good idea to not accept these kinds of requests.

**Ask for proof of identity and Google search anyone you have not personally verified.** It's easy for someone to portray a false self if you do not ask too many questions. If you have not met someone in person and you are only talking to them on the phone, make sure you request a video chat. Scammers, especially those trying to get money from you, may give you a correct photo of themselves and may also video chat with you. Just like the story of Grace and Gary, you may think you have met the perfect match online and then find out later that they possess dark secrets and are not who they claim to be. Therefore, it is important to always be vigilant.

These days, it is easy to find information about people with a quick Internet search. If you meet someone on a dating app and start a relationship, send them a friend request on Twitter, Facebook, TikTok, or Instagram if they have a profile. Always meet them in person and don't delay that, if possible. Meet their friends and family and see where they live. If someone will not show you their home or let you meet their people, that is a red flag.

**Never, ever, give your money to someone you have not met or barely know.** This one might sound super obvious but don't ever do this. *Ever.*

**Make sure your privacy settings are stringent.** A predator will not hesitate to use any information about you against you. The less a stranger knows about you, the better. Make sure you are familiar with your privacy settings and give strangers as little access as possible to anything about your life. This can be as simple as adjusting all your social media accounts to private and not having a public account. On Twitter, that would look like "protecting your tweets," which turns your account to private so only people you accept as followers can see what you post.

**Trust your instincts.** I am a firm believer that our gut instinct is the most powerful tool we have in assessing danger, especially when it comes to predatory people. I often refer people to the book *The Gift of Fear: Survival Signals That Protect Us from Violence*[80] by Gavin de Becker to glean a more complete picture on how to hone our gut instincts and help protect ourselves from dangerous situations and people.

# PROTECTING OURSELVES FROM NARCISSISTIC, LOVE-BOMBING PREDATORS

Narcissists are visual creatures. Social media, with its abundance of photographs, is a perfect hunting ground for them, where they can easily target their unsuspecting victims. Because narcissistic people are so shallow and obsessed with being the best and how other people view them, who they have on their arm is of the utmost importance for their image. By now many of us have heard the phrase "sliding into your DMs (direct messages)," and while totally normal and healthy relationships can start in the DMs, some narcissistic types may be lurking in there as well.

Examining some of the unintentionally narcissistic behaviors that we all may engage in from time to time is beneficial, but it is also important to understand some of the behaviors the more dangerous narcissists on social media engage in so we can better protect ourselves and those we love from falling victim to them. Some of the signs displayed by a narcissistic predator on social media that we can look out for are:

**Love-bombing.** If someone is over the top and telling you how amazing you are without ever having met you in person and not knowing much about you, that could be an immediate warning signal. Predatory narcissists use flattery, over-the-top gestures, and grand proclamations of adoration to win over a target. It is often the only strategy they have. Keep your guard up if someone seems a little too overbearing or effusive right out of the gate.

**Boundary violations/anger/possessiveness.** In many cases, even in the beginning stages of getting to know someone, a narcissistic predator will push boundaries. If you say no to something, they may get upset and try to convince you to say yes. They will usually keep pushing, no matter how many times you stand your ground. Regardless of whether someone doing this is a narcissist or not, this is always a huge red flag. People who do not respect boundaries to that degree almost never get better. In fact, it usually gets much worse.

Narcissistic types online also might get angry if you reject them or if they assume you are rejecting them (narcissistic rage). Any kind of anger that comes out of nowhere, or from you putting up a boundary, will also almost certainly get worse. Usually, a narcissist will lash out if they feel emotionally injured. You may feel very unsettled after an interaction like this. A narcissist knows this and will either pretend nothing happened, or they will act as sweet as pie and become fun-loving, warm, and loving again. This is where people get thrown off. They will write off an outburst like this and assume the narcissistic person was having a bad day or a bad moment. Once you see the cycle happening—the Jekyll and Hyde behavior that vacillates between angry outbursts and adoring behavior—in a continuous pattern, it's time to move on.

You may get inklings of jealousy and possessiveness from narcissists when you are first getting to know them online. For example, they want to know your schedule, they don't want you spending time with other people, and they want to monopolize your time. If you say that you can't chat right now because you have plans with friends, they might respond, "You don't need to see them; all you need is me!" This might seem cute or flattering at first, but it can be a sign that you can expect even more controlling and abusive behavior further down the road.

**Online behavior that provokes an emotional response from you.** Narcissists are often antagonistic and like to provoke jealousy, hurt, and emotion from their victims. In the words of narcissism expert and bestselling author Shahida Arabi:

> Narcissists enjoy pitting people against one another and that includes using social media to provoke jealousy in their partners; they may do so by flirting with others online, "liking" and following sexually explicit accounts, or even starting secret affairs with strangers . . . If you notice a narcissist frequently flirting with or engaging with dubious material online even while they have a significant other, you may just be spotting a major red flag of their character.[81]

If you are dating or in a relationship with someone and you have discussed their online habits and behaviors that are troubling or bothersome to you and they mock or dismiss your concerns, you may be with someone who has narcissistic traits or even is a full-blown narcissist.

Narcissists love to mock others' pain and exploit their weaknesses. Because they feel entitled, they may up the ante and engage in online behavior that upsets you to provoke a further reaction. This gives them a feeling of control and power over you, while you are completely blindsided and distraught. Depending on the extent or severity of this behavior, seeking couples or individual therapy might be helpful. If the person cannot or will not change this behavior, finding the strength to leave someone like this is critical to avoid long-term damage to yourself.

Don't hesitate to take action if you experience several or all of the examples listed above. These red flags mean the person you are with is dangerous, manipulative, and abusive with the potential to destroy your life. Even one of these signs may warrant your attention and evaluation. You deserve to be treated with love, respect, and care. Those who are highly narcissistic are often incapable of this, even with the help of professionals.

# TIPS, TAKEAWAYS, AND FOOD FOR THOUGHT

1. Do you and your partner ever have arguments about the time spent posting/reading social media posts or the content of your posts?

2. How often do you and your partner spend time on social media? Is social media use by either of you an issue in your relationship? Are there any serious changes (like limiting social media use or cutting back) either of you should make for the greater good of the relationship as it pertains to your social media use?

3. If you are single, have you ever had a bad feeling about the posts of a new love interest on social media? Did your gut turn out to be right?

4. If you think you might be in a relationship with a narcissistic person, what types of behaviors do they engage in on social media that are harmful to you? Have you spoken to them about it? Do they have empathy for your concerns?

# Chapter 6

# KIDS ON SOCIAL MEDIA: ARE WE HARMING OUR CHILDREN AND RAISING NARCISSISTS?

Parenting during the age of social media is confusing and incredibly hard to navigate for many reasons. Parents struggle with if they should share images or anecdotes about their children and, if so, how often and how much detail. In the news, we hear about how social media use is having a negative impact on the mental health of the youth (the focus has recently been on adolescent girls), and we struggle with how to navigate if, when, and how our children should use social media. With seductive content across all platforms, including sexy dances on TikTok and highly curated selfies bombarding us 24/7, many wonder if we are encouraging vanity and narcissism in young people. We are worried about the addictive nature of social media and gaming, the predators that may be lurking online, and how we may be able to protect children if they should encounter them.

All of the above relate to narcissism and are extremely valid concerns. It is what we should be thinking about when it comes to what we share online about our children, what our children may be exposed to on social media, and what this all means in terms of long-term impact on mental health. This chapter will explore these themes and hopefully provide some guidance and insight so that parents are informed to make the decisions that work best for them and their families.

## "SHARENTING" AND SOCIAL MEDIA NARCISSISM

The risks of "sharenting" or "oversharenting," defined as posting many photos, videos, or other information about your children on social media without their consent, has been explored by many experts in the legal, medical, and social science fields. The most obvious and worrisome dangers of sharenting are when unassuming parents find out that innocent images of their children have been stolen and posted on child pornography websites.

Speaking to the Huffington Post, a woman in Utah tells how she stumbled upon images of herself and her eight- and nine-year-old children on at least eleven different pornography sites: "I seriously feel like the worst mom having put these on (social media) and seeing what happened," she said. "I didn't feel that posting family photos could turn into something like that."[82] They had apparently been pulled from her Facebook page and posted on Instagram, with false captions about her daughter's age and sexual orientation, and with hashtags linking to porn sites. She even had her privacy settings set to "only friends," but even that can be problematic; children's online images can still be stolen and used on the Internet with nefarious intent. Unfortunately, images that are considered public are not protected under the law of the Children's Online Privacy Protection Act,[83] which imposes requirements on websites or online services directed to children under thirteen years of age.

Other problematic issues related to sharenting are data theft, public embarrassment, identity violation, and privacy violations. In the Netherlands, a grandmother was sued by her daughter for posting pictures of her grandchildren, even after her daughter (the mother of the children) repeatedly asked her to take them down. The complaint was filed under the General Data Protection Regulation (GDPR), which applied because the posting on Facebook made the photos available to a wider audience. The court ruled in favor of the mother, and the grandmother was forced to delete the Facebook photos.[84] Of course, the Internet is forever—once posted, any photos or material is still "out there" and can be accessed by anyone who is determined enough.

Anyone who is a parent understands the temptation of sharing cute photos, milestones, and adorable anecdotes about their children with family and friends. However, social media has created a much bigger beast than anyone can ideally manage, considering many people's friend lists consist of people who would not necessarily be considered close friends. In many cases, people have friends on their list who are casual acquaintances, or even complete strangers. And, depending on your privacy settings, what you post may also be seen by your friends' friends, who may share them, and so on.

While sharenting is an understandable phenomenon, and social media offers an easy and efficient way to share the joys and milestones of our children with the people we care about the most, when does it cross a line and enter narcissistic territory? These are questions that many concerned parents grapple with in the digital age. Parents are torn because they would like to freely share and document their children's milestones electronically, but they also have understandable apprehensions about what this means for their children and what responsibility they have as parents.

While there are definitely narcissistic parents who engage in more than their fair share of sharenting, what are some of the other psychological motivations for sharenting that are not narcissistic? In a research study that looked at millennial parents' motivations for sharenting, the results indicated that the motives were "to receive affirmation and social support, to demonstrate the ability to take care of children, for social participation, and documentation."[85]

Parenting can be difficult and sometimes isolating, so online parenting groups have proven to be an important form of social support and camaraderie. Social media has normalized the common struggles parents face. On the flip side, it has also made parents feel shame and guilt about their parenting choices.

Online groups and blogs can help parents feel less alienated and offer specific advice. They can also help parents feel less alone if they are going through a specific issue related to their children that they might otherwise not easily find in their community. There are support groups for parents who have children with allergies, special needs, cancer and other illnesses, and so much more. These groups can literally be a lifeline for these parents and are an incredible resource for sharing advice and offering support and affirmation.

Other forms of sharenting can at best annoy others and at worst cause damage to the children. In the article "Sharenting: Why Mothers Post About Their Children on Social Media," the authors say, "Sharenting has been heavily criticized as a form of digital narcissism. But more than this, it is also seen as one long parental 'humblebrag.'"[86]

Humblebragging about children and over-posting of the mundane things a child does is often done innocently and obliviously but still has the potential to embarrass the child (especially later in life when they are old enough to see it), violate their privacy, or as seen earlier in the chapter, have their photos and identity stolen and used in harmful and disturbing ways.

Narcissists posting about their children do so without care, empathy, or respect for them. How would we know this? It would be content that the child might find shaming or even horrifying. Konrad Iturbe, a nineteen-year-old software developer from Spain, discovered his parents had been posting photos of him online and told the BBC that:

> He says discovering the pictures felt like a "breach of privacy". It particularly bothered him because there were photos of him as a young child, and his mother's Instagram account was open to the public.
>
> "I didn't want photos of my youth shared, it's a very intimate thing," he says, adding that he is also worried about "facial recognition algorithms" and people being able to "start tracing me when I'm older."[87]

Konrad's parents did the right thing by immediately taking the photos down and respecting his boundaries. The act of sharing without his consent was normal parental pride, and they reacted appropriately when they found that their son was nevertheless troubled. Had they been narcissists, the reaction would have been quite the opposite. He likely would have been mocked, shamed, made to feel guilty, or criticized for making such a request.

## NARCISSISTIC PARENTS ON SOCIAL MEDIA

Narcissistic parents don't hesitate to use social media as another way to cause their teenage or adult children harm, grief, and pain.

Some of these narcissistic behaviors may include addiction to websites like Facebook, spending lots of time taking photos of the family or children, immediately posting the photos and obsessing over the likes and comments, starting fights online, posting content that they believe makes them look morally superior, using social media to make passive-aggressive attacks on their children, constant surveillance of the children and their friends, and lots of other boundary violations.

Children of narcissistic parents will resort to blocking their parents completely or create fake accounts with aliases so their parents do not know how to find them on social media. Many of us can relate to having a family member (or two) who may seem overly intrusive or badgering online, but a narcissistic parent will take it to another level.

In extreme cases, narcissistic parents will obsessively stalk and comment on their child's social media activity, often behind the scenes through text messages. Because they need to control, they will demand the child delete certain posts or ask them to post things that the parent wants to boost their self-image.

A narcissistic parent will also use social media to harass and shame the child through criticism. For instance, "That dress emphasizes your big waist and makes you look awful. You shouldn't be posting that." There will also be excessive guilt-tripping and self-centered comments such as, "You never like any of my posts. Obviously, you don't love me or care about all the sacrifices I have made for you." They may also use their "flying monkeys" to attack or spy on their child on social media.

## Dealing with a Narcissistic Parent Online and Respecting Your Child's Social Media Boundaries

Catering to a narcissistic parent is exhausting. Dealing with their constant boundary violations is grueling and draining, and social media has aggravated and complicated the issues. Navigating a life in the real world can be difficult enough, but with many people having an online life, we now must learn to put up boundaries in both realms.

If you think you may be dealing with a narcissistic parent on social media, muting or blocking, depending on your preference, can help. Asking friends not to engage with a narcissistic parent and blocking the parent's flying monkeys, are other strategies one can use to protect oneself from those who continue to cross boundaries and not listen to requests for privacy and respect. Some people may find deactivating all their social media accounts, at least temporarily, provides them with a much-needed break from all the drama.

Although social media has provided fertile ground for narcissism, it has also provided great support systems for those who have survived any type of narcissistic abuse. Here, victims can put a name to what is happening to them and find solace and support from others who also might have narcissistic parents, family members, romantic partners, colleagues, bosses, and the like.

Sharing, and whom we share with on social media, can be hard to navigate for parents. Having respect for a child's personal boundaries, wishes, and feelings about their digital footprint and social media presence is a great way to be the opposite of a parent with narcissistic traits and behaviors.

Leah Plunkett, author of *Sharenthood: Why We Should Think Before We Talk About Our Kids Online*[88] offered excellent advice regarding sharenting on the Reset podcast:

> While I'm not advocating for parents to become technophobes, I am advocating for us to make values-based decisions and think when we are using a digital technology or service, whether it is social media to

stay connected or an Alexa or other home assistant: Are the benefits from that outweighing the potential privacy risks and the potential downstream risks to children's current and future opportunities?

I don't advocate parents break their phones or go live in a hut in the woods. But I do advocate that we all raise our awareness that there are hidden costs and hidden risks to doing things digitally.[89]

Compassionate parents give deep thought to these questions and make decisions accordingly. There are many well-intentioned, great parents who want the best for their kids and respect their boundaries. I have no doubt they will make thoughtful choices about what they share about their children on social media, especially when they weigh the realities, and potential consequences, of sharing in the age of "no real privacy."

## HOW SOCIAL MEDIA PLATFORMS MONETIZE YOUR POSTS FOR PROFIT

While people who exploit their children reveal the worst parental behavior with regard to sharenting, researcher Priya Kumar believes that the larger problem is the exploitation of parents by social media companies that profit off them. Kumar writes about this topic for *Fast Company*, saying:

Too often, public discourse pits parents against children. Parents, critics say, are being narcissistic by blogging about their kids and posting their photos on Facebook and Instagram; they're willing to invade their child's privacy in exchange for attention and likes from their friends. So the story goes.

But this parent-versus-child framing obscures a bigger problem: the economic logic of social media platforms that exploit users for profit.[90]

Kumar may have a point, and while narcissistic parents' sharenting can cause many issues and damage to their children, we also need to explore the underlying issue, which is the fact that these platforms use business models to mine data from you, only to profit off you.

The issue isn't necessarily only that people want to and do share their children on social media with loved ones, but more so that the big tech companies are knowingly taking advantage of this, and not doing enough to protect people, especially children, from the worst consequences. Recently, Frances Haugen, a data engineer and former employee of Facebook, made headlines by testifying in front of a US Senate subcommittee and going public with internal leaked documents, saying that Facebook knowingly harms children, sows division, and harms democracy. This controversy isn't necessarily surprising to anyone, but it does highlight the exploitation by some of the big tech companies not only of children but also their parents, as Priya Kumar stated above.

## IS SOCIAL MEDIA MAKING OUR KIDS MORE NARCISSISTIC?

Almost every parent I know has major concerns about their children using social media and fear for what this might look like in the future. Many of us joke that we are so glad we didn't grow up with the technology, especially as preteens or teenagers. As we've noted, even adults are not immune from comparing themselves to others online. For an insecure, developing adolescent, this can be a recipe for disaster. Parents have good reason to wonder if living their lives online will negatively impact their children's self-esteem and mental health. Further, will the lack of authentic, face-to-face communication impair their child's ability to empathize, or maybe even make them narcissistic, self-centered, and self-absorbed?

These concerns are valid. We really don't know the long-term effects of nonstop social media use on the developing brain. Most parents have a goal to raise a secure and well-adjusted individual who makes positive contributions to society. Is this possible in today's world?

Dr. Josh Grubbs, a professor at Bowling Green State University who authored a paper titled "Young Adults Distressed by Labels of Narcissism, Entitlement,"[91] told the *New York Times:*

> The widespread belief that young adults are more self-absorbed may have been fueled by the fact that social media has made today's narcissists much easier to find." It could be that social media is making the younger generations more narcissistic, but it could also be that social media is just making a narcissist much easier to find.[92]

Narcissistic personality disorder is theorized by some to emerge from childhood as a response to parents who overvalue them (from the work of Eddie Brummelman et al. at the University of Amsterdam). Their research found that narcissism was predicted by parental overvaluation:

> Children seem to acquire narcissism, in part, by internalizing parents' inflated views of them (e.g., "I am superior to others" and "I am entitled to privileges") . . . These findings uncover early socialization experiences that cultivate narcissism and may inform interventions to curtail narcissistic development at an early age.[93]

This same study also found that parental warmth (attention and affection) predicted higher self-esteem in children. Self-esteem is not to be confused or conflated with narcissism. A narcissist feels superior to others but does not always necessarily like themselves. High self-esteem relates to liking who you are, while also having concern and empathy for others.

In addition to Brummelman's work on how narcissism develops in children, the study "The Apple of Daddy's Eye: Parental Overvaluation Links the Narcissistic Traits of Father and Child" provides further evidence that parental narcissism may influence the development of narcissism in the child and that earlier interventions for both parents and children would be an important step in preventing the further development of narcissism in children.[93A]

There are other theories as to how narcissism begins in childhood, including Otto Kernberg's theory that narcissism begins to develop when a parent is cold, overly critical, and distant. The thought is that the child develops a defense mechanism to protect themselves from the pain of being devalued by the parent, and so they create an internal grandiose self to protect themselves from feeling the pain of not experiencing unconditional love, warmth, and emotional safety.[94]

Both Brummelman and Kernberg's theories have always made sense to me, and both seem to contribute to the development of narcissism. In all the research I have done, parental warmth, acceptance, and unconditional love are the main ingredients within our control when attempting to raise a secure child with positive regard for themselves and others. Parenting that falls somewhere in the sweet spot between not being hypercritical or overindulgent seems to be the best method if we are seeking to avoid raising a child who goes on to develop unhealthy narcissism.

Given that most narcissism is supposed to begin its course in middle-late childhood, it seems more urgent than ever to examine the role social media plays; this is usually the time a child will begin to start using these platforms independently or will have friends doing so.

The good news here is that studies are mixed when it comes to adolescents and the effect social media use has on empathy and narcissism. An article in the *Journal of the American Academy of Pediatrics*[95] noted:

> One study of young adults found that the more time girls spent in front of a screen, the lower their cognitive empathy was.[96] The same study found that more time online was associated with more face-to-face communication among both boys and girls. This study was correlational, making causal inferences difficult. A more recent study that followed teenagers over a one-year period found that those who used social media more at the beginning of the study had higher cognitive and emotional empathy scores one year later.[97]

This finding indicates that social media may be a positive way to develop empathy in youth. Homing in on what aspects of social media encourage empathy and connection will be helpful for instructing parents on the ways they can help their children use it to enhance more positive characteristics and traits that will serve them well in life.

All the news isn't rosy, unfortunately. Dr. Sara Konrath, a researcher on empathy, found that empathy in young people has been declining over the years. According to a study she conducted, American college students self-reported that they were becoming lower in empathy over time. Konrath realized that the decline in empathy was also happening at the same time as a rise in mental health problems with youth and believes that the rising narcissism can be attributed to a culture of burnout. Konrath believes that there is a difference in the reasons for why people are drawn to social media in the first place. She is of the opinion that empathetic people are attracted to it because of the ability to connect with others and use it for different purposes than those who are narcissistic.[98] Narcissistic people will use social media to fulfill their narcissistic needs, and empathetic people will be drawn to it for connection and bonding.

Starting before the teenage years, parents can help teach children how to use social media in an empathetic way when children are old enough to navigate social networking platforms safely. Teenagers often go through tumultuous experiences and use social media to connect with peers. In an ideal world, interventions with parents and children at risk for developing narcissism would utilize therapy and teach social-emotional skills, but we don't live in an ideal world.

Therefore, parents can also help make their children aware and teach them ways to use social media in a beneficial way, while also teaching them how to deal with peers who may have narcissistic tendencies. Narcissistic adolescents, especially when low empathy is involved, are more likely to be aggressive.[99] Obviously, we don't want our children engaging with a narcissistic adolescent with low empathy, but if they were to come across one, knowing how to identify that person and then not engaging with them unless absolutely necessary is important. This will be explored more in the next chapter around cyberbullying.

I spoke to Kaitlin Ugolik Phillips, author of *The Future of Feeling: Building Empathy in a Tech-Obsessed World,*[100] and wanted to know her thoughts on what social media might mean for the younger generations given the overwhelming prevalence of it and the documented rates of declining empathy. She told me:

> My instinct is that it depends on the kid. If you're living and growing up in an environment where you're doing a lot of Social Emotional

Learning (SEL) and it's an empathetic environment, then there is hope. But I think for kids that don't have access to those kinds of relationships and that kind of instruction, it is a problem. One thing that's been fascinating to me, is that especially on places like TikTok you'll see the young kids, like Gen Z and younger—they really seem to get that this social media world we have handed them isn't sustainable. They just seem to understand a lot of the burnout stuff: cyberbullying, lack of empathy, they seem to get it. The way they use these platforms to raise awareness about things, share experiences about mental health, and raise money . . . that is really encouraging to me.

Kaitlin also pointed me toward the work of Michael Kraus of Yale University, who found that voice-only communication enhances empathic accuracy.[101] People who just hear each other had a more empathic response to another person as opposed to seeing and hearing them simultaneously. Kaitlin noted that when she listens to podcasts, she can't respond to them—she can only concentrate and reflect on what she is hearing. She told me, "I encourage people to seek out audio information because it's a better way to digest information, which I think is good for empathy."

This information Phillips shared is encouraging because if we can give our children more content, such as podcasts and audiobooks to listen to, that is one way we may be able to promote empathy in children when it comes to their digital use.

In addition to providing children with more audio content in their digital spaces, what other things can we do to encourage empathy on social media? What are other ways we can protect our kids from narcissism on social media?

**Teach digital citizenship awareness.** Although it's easy to dehumanize someone when you don't know them and only interact with them through a screen, it is a good policy to remind children that there is a real person behind it. Teaching our children that it is not okay to be mean to someone online is a good first step. Of course, it is also important to help children understand about privacy, how to secure their accounts so information cannot be used against them, not to share personal information with others, and how to create strong passwords.

**Help them understand the toxicity of constant comparison on social media.** While this may be obvious, it's important to explicitly let children know before they use social media, and to remind them as they use it, that comparison to others will almost always make us feel bad and that what is portrayed online is often not real. Everyone struggles with something, and it is important to let children and adolescents know that no one's life is perfect.

**Use social media to learn about different people and cultures.** Part of developing empathy for others is the acceptance and celebration of differences. The Internet and social media are wonderful avenues to connect with people from different cultures around the world. Especially in the case of teenagers, social media is a place that can connect them with the struggles in different societies, can make them aware of important world issues, and might also encourage them to fundraise and initiate "hashtag campaigns" for causes they find important.

**Keep most social interactions in-person, if possible.** Writing this book while not fully out of a global pandemic gives me total awareness that in-person social interactions are not something to take for granted and that digital socialization is sometimes necessary to keep us connected. After experiencing this pandemic, social distancing, and periods of quarantining, we collectively learned how detrimental social isolation was for children and how virtual learning was not a substitute for in-person instruction. While some children did better with virtual learning for various reasons, many others became depressed and anxious with the lack of social connection.

While studies on the effects of the pandemic and child mental health are still in the works, preliminary findings indicate that depression and anxiety were prevalent in children throughout the pandemic.[102] Global pandemics notwithstanding, helping your children to nurture the friendships they find fulfilling and important and encouraging those face-to-face interactions will go a long way in learning how to build important connections throughout their lifetimes.

**Encourage CPR: Compassion, Passion, and Responsibility.** W. Keith Campbell, the narcissism expert introduced earlier in the book, tells me he uses the term CPR (Compassion, Passion, Responsibility), when thinking about how to raise children who aren't narcissists, both online and in the real world. He tells me, "I think that passion piece is really important, which is encouraging and supporting your kids in doing what they love to do. I think kids need to have relationships that are loving, and they need to learn stuff on their own, as well as face challenges on their own." Campbell also says that if his children have friends in real life, that he doesn't worry too much about social media.

**Teach kids not to engage with aggressive and cruel people online.** With many children and teenagers engaging in gaming, as well as teenagers frequently using social media, it's inevitable they will come across someone who is mean-spirited, and they may even come across an aggressive bully, and worse, a narcissistic or psychopathic personality type. Knowing how to establish appropriate boundaries is critical for them to have a safer online experience. Let your children know that not responding, disengaging, blocking, unfriending, and the like are totally acceptable and necessary responses to anyone who is treating them with disrespect and cruelty. They should also notify a parent or trusted adult when anything feels too much for them to handle on their own.

## TIPS, TAKEAWAYS, AND FOOD FOR THOUGHT

1. What are your feelings about posting photos of your children on social media (and if you do not have children, either other people doing it, or what you might do regarding your future children)?

2. Do you believe one should not post photos of their children on social media at all, sparingly, or only on private profiles with close friends and family? Why?

3. If you have children, how might you protect their privacy online more? How will you help them use social media if they are of age or when they become old enough to use it?

4. How might you help your children use social media in a way that does not promote narcissistic traits?

# Chapter 7

# CYBERBULLYING, CYBERSTALKING, INTERNET TROLLS, GAMING, MISOGYNY, AND NARCISSISM

## Addison and "Ben": Deadly Deception

Addison, a thirteen-year-old girl, struggled with her self-esteem and her weight. Fueling her insecurity was the negative feedback she got from her Instagram account, which she used frequently, and which allowed her to compare herself with others. She often found posts from her peers, showing photos of themselves having fun together, usually without Addison. This made her feel left out and increased her self-esteem issues.

When a boy named "Ben" requested to follow her on Instagram, including an accompanying direct message, she felt excited. Ben seemed cute from his photo, and she had never received any real interest from a boy before. Ben said he went to another school and the two started chatting frequently online. Ben told Addison she was pretty, and they had many deep conversations, although they never spoke over the phone or met in person. Addison felt she could trust Ben and started revealing deeply personal things to him, including her insecurities about her weight.

Several months after they started their online relationship, Ben sent Addison a devastating message, "This is the end of the line, I'm done."

She replied, "What? I don't understand? What's wrong?"

"I'm done because I'm not a real person." "Ben" went on to say that he was a fake account created by some kids at Addison's school. She was shocked and horrified, thinking of all the things she had shared. What happened in the weeks that followed are the stuff of nightmares. The kids behind the fake account used Addison's personal disclosures against her, taunted her, sent cruel and threatening messages, and even told her she should kill herself. Most of this bullying was done online and through social media as it took on a life of its own. Addison was convinced she could never escape the public shaming and torment. In a devastating, all-too-familiar ending to a tragic story like this, one day her mother discovered her daughter's lifeless body in her family's basement. Addison had hung herself.

No one should ever go through what Addison and her family did. I wish this was a rare story, but all it takes is a quick Internet search to see too many heart-wrenching and crushing stories like this, describing lives completely ruined by cyberbullying.

Various headlines make the news every so often, like when twelve-year-old Mallory Grossman from New Jersey killed herself after being relentlessly harassed by several peers on Snapchat, Instagram, and through text messages.[103] In this case, as in many others, schools, parents of the bullies, and even the legal system fail to do enough to prevent deadly outcomes. Parents of the cyberbullied often feel schools are dismissive of their concerns, and in the worst-case scenarios, they end in the most awful outcome imaginable because interventions are not successful and cyberbullying is not taken as seriously as face-to-face bullying.

My passion for narcissism awareness and education was born mostly out of stories like these—the stories that represent innocent people completely traumatized, harmed, murdered, or driven to suicide by behaviors that are linked to narcissism. I personally find it unconscionable that we live in a society that allows this to happen with little reflection or impetus to change. Bullying and harassment in any context stem from a lack of empathy for another human being.

The word *terrorized* is not overly dramatic to describe the effects that bullying and cyberbullying have on their victims. According to *Broadband Search,* in 2021 alone, 60 percent of teenagers reported being cyberbullied, 87 percent of young people have witnessed cyberbullying online, and the majority of cyberbullying is done (in order) on Instagram, Facebook, and Snapchat.[104] In the *Ditch the Label Annual Bullying Survey of 2017,* it was reported that experiencing cyberbullying resulted in 41 percent of young people developing social anxiety, 37 percent developing depression, 26 percent having suicidal thoughts, 25 percent engaging in self-harm, 14 percent developing an eating disorder, and 9 percent abusing alcohol or drugs.[105] It's not just children and teenagers who are witnessing and experiencing cyberbullying. Adults are as well, with four in ten Americans reporting being on the receiving end of online abuse.[106]

With online abuse and cyberbullying becoming all too common, narcissism has been frequently studied as a predictive factor. Not only has narcissism been positively correlated with cyberbullying, but even more frightening is the fact that the dark triad traits (Machiavellianism, psychopathy, and narcissism) are as well.[107] Going even further than that, sadism, deriving pleasure from inflicting pain on others, has also been found to be related to cyberbullying.[108]

Not surprisingly, some of the darkest personality traits a human can possess have strong links to cyberbullying, and some who engage in cyberbullying also enjoy watching others in pain. Cyberbullying is also linked to low self-esteem,[109] so of course not all who cyberbully are narcissists or psychopaths, but the correlations are there and cannot be ignored. It is also important to mention that low self-esteem can also be a part of the profile of a narcissist, specifically the vulnerable types. One study using an anonymous questionnaire with female Chinese adolescents from eleven to eighteen years old found that covert (or vulnerable) narcissism was positively predictive of cyberbullying, but grandiose narcissism was not.[110]

What might a narcissistic cyberbully look like? Knowing that narcissism is on a spectrum, there may be varying degrees of how dangerous a narcissistic cyberbully is, with the most dangerous being a dark triad type.

Are you or a loved one dealing with a narcissistic cyberbully? Here are the traits and behaviors to look out for:

**Demonstrated lack of empathy and remorse across multiple situations.** Most of the time, narcissistic (or psychopathic) cyberbullies will seem to have little empathy for the person they are bullying. They simply will not care they are hurting another person. Note that psychopaths and narcissists may display "cognitive empathy" in some cases, which is the ability to understand another person's feelings. However, it's not the same thing as "emotional empathy," which is the ability to legitimately *share in the feelings* of another person. Lack of remorse goes hand-in-hand with a lack of empathy. If you don't feel empathy for another person, the chances of feeling remorse for your actions are close to zero. What is deeply troubling is that studies show many cyberbullies do not feel anything for the victims they terrorize.[111]

**Continuity of bad behavior (even after interventions and disciplinary actions).** A dangerous narcissist or psychopath will continue to do what they have always done if they can get away with it. The enjoyment they receive overrides the threat of punishment they might receive; there is no incentive to stop. Causing harm to others is behavior that is second nature to a severe narcissist, and in most cases, they continue damaging others for the entirety of their lives.

**Consistent judgment and shaming.** Narcissistic cyberbullies are incredibly judgmental of others online and will shame them. Narcissists know shame feels awful to most people, and some narcissists (the vulnerable/covert type) feel deep shame themselves, so they will weaponize it and use shaming to hurt their targets.

**Unrelenting cruelty.** Cyberbullies thrive on cruelty. When they attack their victims, their ire is deeply intentional, targeted, and especially harsh. If someone says, "Why don't you just kill yourself?" or any variation of that statement, that's a major red flag about the kind of person you are dealing with. You will need to take every possible action you can to protect yourself or your loved one (especially children and adolescents) from their abuse.

**Manipulation and victim blaming.** Narcissists regularly manipulate situations to exert control or shift blame to avoid accountability. When confronted, the person will most likely shift the blame and gaslight—making the victim feel like they are blowing things out of proportion, overly sensitive, and that they are to blame for the harassment.

**Sense of entitlement.** There is literally a definition for an "entitlement cyberbully":

> Entitlement bullies are individuals who believe they are superior and have the right to harass or demean others, especially if the person is different. Targets of entitlement bullies are individuals who are picked on because bullies believe that they are different or inferior.[112]

Because entitlement is a major trait and behavior of a narcissist, a narcissistic cyberbully will most definitely possess a sense of entitlement. A narcissist will often never apologize, so if they are in a situation where they are being held accountable for their behavior at work or school, they will not offer an apology, or they will offer a disingenuous apology that will feel hollow and forced. Sometimes narcissists will also make phony apologies as part of their manipulation, but often once you have dealt with a narcissist enough times, you'll be fully aware that any apologies are insincere.

## WHAT IF YOUR CHILD IS THE CYBERBULLY?

It can be very upsetting as a parent to learn that your child is doing the cyberbullying. Don't assume your child is a narcissist or a budding psychopath and panic, but it is important to address the situation and try to get to the root of it. The Cyberbullying Research Center has some good tips, some of which are summarized here[113]:

1. **Calmly address the issue.** If your child feels they can talk openly to you, you may get the full story. Even if you are hearing something you may not like from your child, remember to talk about it as a behavior and not something that is inherently wrong with the child. If the situation was brought up to you by the school or

another parent, you may start by asking your child to tell you the events as they recall them. You can ask clarifying questions, and if you know they may have left something out, you can bring that up. When you talk about something as a behavior, that would look like: "Hey Charlie, that wasn't very nice when you sent Adam those mean messages on Instagram." You are not saying Charlie isn't nice, but you are labeling the behavior or action as not nice.

2. **Take charge to try and rectify the situation or stop the bullying.** This may involve getting the school involved to help mediate or deleting or temporarily removing your child's social media accounts. How long you may temporarily put an account on pause would depend on what you think is appropriate given the severity of the situation. You can also confiscate your child's phone or devices if need be. You may also want to urge your child to make an apology to whomever they were bullying.

3. **Have your child try to take some ownership by using empathy.** If your child can imagine how the child on the receiving end of the bullying might feel and can feel remorse about it, it may help stop the urge to be a bully. The goal is to understand that bullying, no matter what the circumstance, is never okay or acceptable, and there are other alternatives to dealing with relational problems. Ask your child to imagine how they would feel if they were on the receiving end of the bullying.

4. **Seek the help of a child psychologist or therapist who may be able to get to the root of the issue and offer strategies to cope.** If you feel that the behavior or situation is unmanageable or overwhelming, do not be afraid to get a professional involved. There may be underlying anxiety or perhaps another issue that the therapist should be trained to help identify and treat accordingly.

# CYBERSTALKING AND NARCISSISM

## Wes: The Never-Ending Date from Hell

Sophia had only been on a few dates with Wes when she decided to end things with him. There was something about him that she found slightly controlling and rigid. They had met online through a dating app, and Wes had been super intense from the start. He wanted to spend all their time together and would get annoyed if Sophia had other plans.

After gently telling Wes that she did not think there was a connection between them, Wes told Sophia she would regret ending things with him. Sophia felt unnerved but relieved she was rid of Wes. Or so she thought.

When she logged on to her Facebook and Instagram accounts the next day, she discovered hundreds of upsetting messages: "You're a whore," and "What a slut, you'll sleep with anyone," and "How do you squeeze all that fat into your jeans?" and "You'll never find anyone to date, let alone marry you." She immediately blocked Wes but would then get messages from random social media accounts belonging to strangers, and she knew he was behind them all.

Wes had also managed to find out who her friends were, most likely from when he had access to viewing her social media accounts before she blocked him. He messaged a few of them, spreading lies that Sophia had told him terrible things about them and to stay away from her. They knew the truth and didn't buy it, but when those friends blocked Wes, he became consumed with anger and upped the ante on his vengeance. He moved on to contacting Sophia's boss, colleagues, and even former employers. He sent them fake, pornographic nude pictures of Sophia in compromising positions, Photoshopping her head on someone else's body.

In a shocking move that Sophia never expected, Wes filed a police report against her, saying that she was stalking and harassing him! As evidence, he presented violent and angry emails that he alleged were from Sophia after he somehow managed to hack into one of her older e-mail accounts that she no longer used. There was not much Sophia could do. It was a he-said, she-said situation, and anyone who has unfortunately been there and done that knows that there is often very little law enforcement or restraining orders can do in these situations.

Eventually, the harassment stopped. After months without any online attacks from Wes, Sophia believes he has moved on from her and found a new target. It's impossible for her to simply move on with her life after this much emotional damage. The trauma is still very much present for her, and she lives in fear. Text messages, phone calls, and even checking her e-mail scare her because she is always afraid that she will hear from Wes, or someone will call her and tell her he did something to try and ruin her reputation.

## CYBERSTALKING NARCISSISTS

Cyberstalking is the use of electronic communications to harass, stalk, frighten, demean, humiliate, and slander with the purpose to hurt another person. The motivations behind cyberstalking are usually revenge or an attempt to control someone else. Cyberstalking can also be done in tandem with stalking that is done offline. In cases where the stalking is done after the end of a relationship, it can progress to physical harm, intimate partner violence, and in the most tragic cases, murder.

Amie Harwick, a popular sex therapist based in Los Angeles, was one example of a beautiful and bright life snuffed out by a violent and vengeful stalker. During her relationship with Gareth Pursehouse, Harwick had to file multiple restraining orders, writing in one that he had, on various occasions, punched her; slammed her head into the ground; pulled her out of a car, giving her a bloody nose, and then left her on a freeway. These were just a few instances of the physical abuse she endured.

Pursehouse also cyberstalked and harassed Amie, sending her threatening texts saying, "Things will get worse." Beyond that, every few years she would find cruel and anonymous posts about herself on a message board (although she could not prove that it was him and had a former friend who could also be behind those messages).[114]

One evening, Harwick ran into Pursehouse at an event, where he became very agitated and angry upon seeing her. Harwick tried to use her training as a therapist to deescalate the situation, but later that evening, he showed up where she lived, strangled her, and threw her off a balcony to her death.

Cyberstalking and intimate partner cyberstalking are strongly associated with narcissistic, psychopathic, and dark triad traits. A study exploring the gender differences of intimate partner cyberstalking found that:

> Controlling relationship behaviors was a significant predictor of intimate partner cyberstalking. Further, gender (women), vulnerable narcissism, direct sadism (verbal and physical), and secondary psychopathy were significant, positive predictors of intimate partner cyberstalking. Importantly, significant gender differences appeared regarding predictors; vulnerable narcissism and direct verbal sadism were significant predictors for women, and only secondary psychopathy was a significant predictor for men.[115]

In a review of twenty-six studies on the relationship of dark personality traits and anti-social online behavior, most anti-social online behavior is associated with the dark triad, with psychopathy being most related, followed by Machiavellianism and sadism, and narcissism with the least association out of all the traits.[116]

## PROTECTING YOURSELF FROM CYBERSTALKERS

The associations between the most dangerous personality traits and cyberstalking are perhaps most terrifying because the horrific stories could happen to anyone. Moreover, people go through hell trying to rid themselves of online stalkers. Because there are now so many online channels on which to communicate, and since information is so readily available on the Internet, victims feel powerless to stop someone who relentlessly goes after them. However, there are things you can do to make it harder for a narcissist or psychopath to take your personal information to use against you, or to stalk and harass you (or your loved ones).

Below are a few ways to protect yourself from a past, present, or future cyberstalker:

**Never accept friend requests from strangers or share any personal information online.** I would make this a hard rule—with no exceptions—especially when talking to youth about social media safety. This can help prevent a random cyberstalker from having access to you or your loved ones. Some cases of cyberstalking have started with a random friend request from a stranger or distant acquaintance and quickly escalated. Also, never share any identifiable personal information online (names of family, pets, address, phone number, etc.), or have any of it public in your profiles. Sometimes our personal information is public and that is not in our control, and in those cases, we just have to do what we can.

**Build a firewall with privacy settings and password changes.** Go into your privacy settings and turn off location services. Change passwords frequently, do not use the same password for different accounts, and when you do formulate a password make sure it's long and composed of upper- and lowercase letters, numbers, and special characters. These elements usually make for very strong passwords, and some apps can suggest them for you and store them in a secure place. According to Norton, you can buy software security programs to help prevent someone from installing spyware on your devices and to delete or make private any public calendars or itineraries.[117]

**Avoid using your full name on social media profiles.** Some people want to be accessible so others can find them. If you want more privacy and are selective about what you share and with whom, it might be worthwhile to use a variation of your name or an alias on your social media profiles that only your close friends and family know.

## HOW TO PROTECT YOURSELF IF YOU ARE BEING CYBERSTALKED

If someone is making you uncomfortable, or you feel unsafe, here are some things you can do to make it harder for them to stalk you online:

**Report right away.** *Fightcyberstalking.org* recommends reporting the incidents to local law enforcement or filing a complaint with the FBI Internet Crime Complaint Center. Make sure you save and print out where possible all the harassment (texts, social media messages, voicemails, e-mails, etc.).

**Block or delete social media accounts and e-mail addresses.** Blocking is always a good step if you are dealing with any type of harassment. However, if things become too much for you to handle, don't hesitate to change your phone number, delete and get a new e-mail address, and delete your social media accounts. You can always create new accounts with a name that is not identifiable, and going forward only use them with the most trusted people in your circles.

**Move if you must.** It's unfortunate when this happens, but I know of several people who had to physically move to protect themselves from a dangerous person who knew where they lived. Do whatever you have to do to feel safe. Even if people think you are paranoid, your safety and sense of security and peace of mind in your own home is more important than anything else.

**Tell people what is happening and seek support.** Don't go through something like this alone. Tell your trusted people—family and friends—what is happening and make sure someone always knows your whereabouts (you can find out how to use emergency location sharing with only those you trust with a quick Internet search). Don't hesitate to also seek support from counselors and groups.

# THE SECRET LIFE OF INTERNET TROLLS

## Terra's Story: A Nurse Doxxed and Trolled for Trying to Help Others

Terra Kater, a nurse practitioner in Florida, has been working on the frontlines during the pandemic. After everything she had seen during the pandemic, she felt she couldn't sit back and do nothing about the misinformation she was seeing on social media. At first, she started her account anonymously and called herself @wooanonwarrior as a way to combat misinformation and conspiracies about the pandemic. Unfortunately, Terra was not able to stay anonymous for long, telling me:

> I was pointing out specific accounts that were spreading misinforma-
> tion, and that was when the doxxing began. Someone shared my name,
> my old address, my NPI and license numbers, where my husband
> worked, and then sent his 50,000 followers to harass me. I did contact
> the FBI. I spoke with someone, but I have never heard if anything came
> of it. This person that doxxed me still has his social media account even
> though his accounts have been deleted twenty-nine times.

Being harassed by trolls and doxxed (when someone publishes your private information for malicious purposes or revenge) took a toll on Terra's mental health. She had to initially make some changes to protect herself:

> I scaled back for some time. I said I wasn't going to talk about COVID or the vaccine for some time. But after the support of my followers that I have met, and also many of the other science communicators, I just can't let these people silence me. I am doing nothing wrong. I am discussing COVID education and helping to debunk misinformation.

After her experience, Terra is angry, noting that cyberbullies and trolls are not held accountable. She has been harassed daily and sometimes relentlessly, cruelly taunted and critiqued by angry trolls. The type of abuse she has received is heinous and inexcusable. When she describes some of the messages she has received, it immediately made me recoil in horror:

> I do not believe cyberbullies are held accountable. The abuse, death threats, being called a Nazi, telling me I'm abusing my kids for getting them vaccinated, making fun of me in general with fat-phobic comments almost daily; no one is held accountable for that. Even the guy that doxxed me. He's still going. Still spreading conspiracies, hate speech, vaccine misinformation and more. It's beyond frustrating.

After all this abuse online, why would Terra choose to bravely continue her social media account, especially when she no longer chooses to be anonymous? No one could blame her for deleting her social media account and going offline forever after her experience. For this dedicated nurse and educator, ultimately the good outweighs the bad. She has met some amazing people, including her followers, and others like herself who are widely known as science communicators (most often doctors, nurses, epidemiologists, immunologists, etc.). She feels a real bond with them and hopes to meet them in real life at some point. At the end of the day, Terra feels she is making a difference and says she is just trying to make the world a better place for everyone.

We've all read posts from Internet trolls: those who write inflammatory or incendiary content online with the intent of evoking a negative reaction from other people. They're active in comment fields everywhere—from news sites to message boards. Some comment anonymously or with a fake screenname that doesn't identify who they are (although most sites now try to prevent that) but there are those who have identifiable screennames and troll with little shame or fear of consequences. The comments and behavior are usually extreme; trolls are cruel, vulgar, and full of hate and rage. Insulting, lying, and spewing hate—whether anonymously or incognito—is a way trolls unleash their animosity and ruthlessness on others.

Like cyberstalking, it should come as no surprise that those who troll on the Internet have very high levels of sadism along with the other dark triad traits. The 2014 study, "Trolls Just Want to Have Fun," found that trolling is highly correlated with psychopathy and Machiavellianism.[118]

The anonymity of "keyboard warriors" can breed empathy issues. The context makes it much easier for them to say something blunt, harsh, or cruel because there are no consequences and they cannot see the other person they attack, which makes it easier to dehumanize them. All it takes is someone having a bad day or going through a hard time to lash out anonymously at another anonymous person and become a version of a troll.

W. Keith Campbell added, "Anonymity gives you protection to do what you want, and when you're anonymous, you're also more swayed by the herd."

Anonymity is not all bad, though, and can also be a good thing online—it can provide a safe space for someone to seek support for something they feel they cannot otherwise share. A good policy for anonymously posting online is to ask yourself how you would feel if your identity was discovered. (This does not apply to sharing something deeply personal or private online, although you should consider this, too, for privacy reasons, as nothing is fully safe on the Internet.) Before you post something that is snarky or mean-spirited or offer an opinion on someone that you know would be hurtful to them, ask yourself how you would feel if your identity were revealed for all to see. If the answer is, "I'd be ashamed," or "I would feel humiliated if anyone knew I was behind this" then *do not post it*—the Golden Rule notwithstanding. Trolling has no point other than to unleash misdirected anger at a person who does not deserve it, and create ill will and damage to someone else, lasting far beyond the time it took to unleash the tirade.

As the wise meme and Internet adage goes, "Don't feed the trolls." Although ignoring trolls will not necessarily put a complete stop to their bad behavior, what they really want is a reaction from you. The more emotional reactions they get, the more they will get a thrill and a sense of power. Engaging trolls online just gives them more fuel for their fire—and narcissistic supply. If you ignore a troll who incessantly posts on one topic, eventually they will stop, even if just because they've moved on to their next trolling project. (If it doesn't stop, see the previous section on cyberstalking.)

## GAMING SAFETY AND PROTECTION

If you or your children are gaming, you're likely to come across at least a few narcissistic personalities. Vulnerable narcissism has been found to predict problematic gaming,[119] and there is insidious racism and bullying that tends to seep into the gaming and online role-playing world. A *Wired* article, "How 'Roblox' Became a Playground for

Virtual Fascists,"[120] discusses the problem Roblox—a global gaming platform—has with far-right extremists who use antisemitic language and even go as far as Nazi role-playing.

Shockingly, there were two Roblox re-creations of the Christchurch Mosque shootings in New Zealand (they have since been taken down) and other racist themes that can be designed and used to slowly groom children by normalizing extremist ideology. While there is not a lot of data about how Roblox or similar games can be used to radicalize people, it is important to be aware that this does happen, and children don't have the capacity to fully understand how the game is promoting hateful and dangerous ideologies.

Teaching your children how to block and report, especially by taking screenshots of offensive messages, is important to help protect them against vulnerable narcissistic bullies looking to provoke and agitate. Just as with adults, children should never include personal information in their usernames and should likewise never give personal information to anyone. Make sure your child's webcam is covered (cybercriminals can use webcams to hack or gather footage to extort or blackmail), and teach your children about online predators and how they should always be skeptical of strangers they play games with online.

Predators and pedophiles may use games and pose as underage players to target children. Former FBI agent Brad Garret told ABC News:

> Once they (online predators and pedophiles) feel comfortable, they get them to switch to Facebook or fill-in-the blank social media where they are not talking over the gaming system. Once they get (pictures) they have them from a blackmail standpoint . . . "I want more explicit

pics. If you do not send me more, I will release these to your school and so forth."[121]

Being aware for yourself and teaching your children how predators might use social media to harm others is a good first step in protection from narcissists, and even worse, psychopaths and sadists online.

## VICTIM BLAMING AND NARCISSISM

Victim blaming—when the victim of a crime or a wrongful act is held partially or fully responsible for what happened to them—is another type of online abuse that is usually perpetrated by people with dark triad traits. Several studies have found that observers of online abuse usually blame victims on the receiving end of the abuse.[122] One study examining celebrity abuse on Twitter found that narcissism predicted increased victim blame of celebrities who were experiencing online abuse.[123] Further elaborating on this study, subsequent research found that sadism also predicted victim blaming as it relates to online abuse.[124]

These studies make perfect sense because the very nature of victim blaming is entrenched in a sense of unwarranted superiority. If someone blames another person for the horrible things that have happened to them, they are implying the victim must have done something to deserve it; this same fate would not have befallen them, they reason, because they are superior and would have made wiser choices. This terribly flawed thinking not only lacks empathy but also excuses the indefensible and depraved behavior of those who commit wrongful acts of rape, murder, stalking, harassment, abuse, and other types of harm.

Dr. Jessica Taylor, author of *Why Women Are Blamed for Everything: Exploring the Victim Blaming of Women Subjected to Violence and Trauma,* wrote:

> I sometimes feel like no matter who the woman or girl is, what she did, what she said, where she's from—we still find a way to blame her for everything that was done to her by an abusive man. I have heard women and girls held responsible for everything from being harassed in the street to being trafficked around the UK and sold to men. This is to the point where women can be murdered by men, and as a society, and as professionals, we still look for what the woman did wrong, what she could have done differently, and why she didn't tell someone what was being done to her.[125]

Ironically, Dr. Taylor herself received thousands of abusive messages with rape and death threats. She also had her computer hacked by a group of organized online trolls right before her book was published, further proving the serious problem of dark triad trolls and abusers online.[126]

Of course, men and boys can be subject to victim blaming as well, but much of it is specifically directed at women. I witnessed this type of online victim blaming when I researched, wrote, and published a book about a family annihilation in Colorado, *My Daddy Is a Hero: How Chris Watts Went from Family Man to Family Killer.* Chris Watts murdered his pregnant wife Shanann and their two young daughters with his bare hands. He stuffed the daughters' bodies in oil tanks and buried Shanann and their unborn son in a shallow grave, later claiming he felt "no remorse" for what he had done.

This particular case had such a high volume of victim blaming directed at Shanann that even the Netflix documentary about the case,

*American Murder,*[127] included how atrocious the victim blaming was. Some of the vitriol centered around themes such as *if only she hadn't "emasculated" her husband, or if only she wasn't so controlling, maybe she and her children would be alive today.*

We are all flawed, as was Shanann, but no one deserves this fate. Chris Watts is a narcissistic psychopath who wanted her and the children gone so he could start a new life with another woman. There is absolutely nothing that justifies domestic violence or brutal murder. Victim blaming changes the narrative, taking the focus off where it should be: on the perpetrator and their actions, for which they should be held fully accountable. It takes a very depraved human to murder his own children and callously submerge their bodies in crude oil. There are no other circumstances that would ever provide any explanation or reasoning for that, barring extreme psychosis, hallucinations, and delusions.

Some may turn to victim blaming to control their own anxieties about feeling powerless in a world that can often seem unjust and unfair. They often erroneously believe bad things won't happen to them if they can attribute blame to the victim. Using twisted logic, they convince themselves they can avoid the same fate and generally protect themselves from anything bad happening to them.

The truth is, bad things will visit all of us at some point or another. Some of the worst suffering in the world will never make sense. Unfortunately, online forums and anonymity have made it easier to blame those who are already suffering, with posters saying horrible, false things about victims and their loved ones with little accountability. It's yet another form of detachment and dehumanization.

Our society needs to work on this issue, which happens all too frequently. When you see this happening online, refuse to participate in it. Call it out for what it is and replace it with a more empathic response.

## MISOGYNY: HATRED FOR WOMEN

Rejection is a major trigger for narcissistic rage, and many narcissistic men want to punish those they believe have rejected them. The hostility is increased when it comes to women.

Scott Keiller from Kent State University conducted research finding that narcissistic men (95 percent white in this study) are more hostile toward straight women, and that hostility is not equivalent to other groups. Additionally, he found that narcissistic men have more favorable attitudes toward lesbian women.[128] This is because a straight male narcissist feels a huge amount of anger toward a straight woman who rejects him. Cyberstalking is related to rage over rejection, entitlement, and misogyny. A narcissistic man believes he is entitled to a woman—sexually, or otherwise—and feels deep inadequacy and resentment when he is not recognized or given what he believes he deserves. This misogynistic narcissism also translates to victim blaming of women and reveals a deep contempt for them, especially by those they believe have rejected them. As such, they believe that women deserve the suffering that is inflicted upon them.

Keiller said that narcissistic men view women as:

> . . . conniving gold diggers, as teases who tempt men with sex and don't deliver, or as seductresses with plans to trick men and "get them under their thumb." Narcissistic men hold overtly hostile, adversarial ideas about women.

In Keiller's work, he also found that only lesbians escaped the narcissistic rage, perhaps for being eroticized by straight men, and that gay men receive animosity from narcissistic men, but not more so than straight men.[129]

Individual narcissistic men can hold deeply misogynistic beliefs, but misogyny is also a major issue with collective narcissists (the belief that the in-group is more exceptional than the out-group and not sufficiently recognized). Agnieszka Golec de Zavala, the social psychologist and researcher on collective narcissism introduced earlier in the book, told me that she believes "incels" (an online subculture of men who are involuntarily celibate because they cannot find a female romantic or sexual partner) are collectively narcissistic:

> Incels are a community, and they think about themselves as a community. Revenge is a very important motivator in narcissistic narration, revenge in the name of the group, for all the affronts the group is experiencing.

She also mentioned that with respect to their gender, men who are collective narcissists feel the emancipation of women is threatening what they believe is "theirs," and they believe they deserve women, just like they deserve breathing.

Golec de Zavala also told me that her research has found that when vulnerable narcissists get together to vent or preach to each other, it doesn't alleviate the narcissism, but rather makes them more likely to develop collective narcissism. She has also seen that when you expose people to collective narcissistic narration, their vulnerable narcissism increases.

The combination of vulnerable narcissism and collective narcissism and how they may play off each other is concerning. The "group think" helps the justification of the misogyny, entitlement, exploitation, and lack of empathy toward women, and has resulted in horrific mass shootings (such as the Elliot Rodger shooting in Isla Vista California that left six people dead and fourteen injured; he had been targeting sororities), with toxic masculinity as a major part of the motivation.[130]

Cyberbullying, cyberstalking, trolling, victim-blaming, and misogyny are some of the most troubling aspects of social media culture, with most people either experiencing or witnessing any combination of them as social media users. The connections with narcissism, the dark triad, and sadism are troubling, and that is why we need to know if we are dealing with anyone exhibiting these traits. The best thing to do is to stay as far away from them as possible and do whatever it takes to keep these callous predators from causing harm to us or to the people who matter most to us.

## TIPS, TAKEAWAYS, AND FOOD FOR THOUGHT

1. Have you noticed your child becoming upset after spending time online on social media sites? Do you believe they might be victims of cyberbullying? Questions you may want to ask them are: Has anyone ever sent you a message that made you upset online? Are you concerned if anyone has written something mean about you online? Has anyone ever written something mean about you online? If yes, how did you handle it? If your child answers yes to any of these questions, please refer back to cyberbullying prevention tips in this chapter.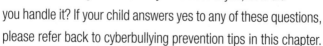

2. Have you been the victim of abusive behavior online from anonymous trolls or bullies? How have you tried to protect yourself

from this? If you have not done so already, what sort of protective boundaries around social media can you create?

3. Have you posted abusive, hurtful, or cruel things anonymously online? Have you harassed someone on social media before? If so, why did you do it and what was the point of it? What will you do the next time someone says something with which you disagree?

4. If you have an urge to post something hurtful about someone, or if someone asks you to post something hurtful about someone else, refrain from doing it.

5. If you are posting on social media anonymously, ask yourself, Would I post the same thing if my name was attached to this? If the answer is, no, refrain from posting it, unless it is something that is helpful (for example, reporting abusive online behavior when you see it).

# Chapter 8

# POLITICS, RACISM, BIG TECH, AND NARCISSISM

*"The ugliest government is the one which is spreading fear to its own people. The finest government is the one which encourages its own people to criticize the government harshly."*
—Mehmet Murat Ildan

## POLITICIANS, WORLD LEADERS, AND NARCISSISM ON SOCIAL MEDIA

The merging of social media with politics has been both interesting, challenging, and even worrisome. President Donald Trump became the first politician to wield the medium unrelentingly. He was frequently labeled the poster child for social media narcissism, with his infamous and often incendiary tweets prompting criticism from all sides of the political spectrum. He received an unofficial diagnosis of narcissistic personality disorder from multiple groups of psychologists and psychiatrists, breaking the infamous Goldwater Rule, which prohibits members of the American Psychiatric Association from diagnosing a public figure who they have not examined in person, and if said person has not consented to their mental health records being made available for public consumption. Eventually, Trump's niece, Mary Trump (a clinical psychologist), wrote a book[131] of her own, calling her uncle a "textbook narcissist."

Narcissistic politicians are not a new topic of discussion, and when exploring their convergence, it doesn't mean that all (or even most) politicians have NPD. However, someone seeking a high-level office or a position with legitimate power inevitably will have higher degrees of narcissism than the general population. The late Jerrold M. Post, MD wrote in his book *Narcissism and Politics: Dreams of Glory*[132]:

> The epidemic of individuals with significant narcissistic traits seems to have reached pandemic proportions among politicians. This is not to say that all politicians are narcissistic, but the arena of public service and its limelight is particularly attractive, indeed irresistible, to individuals with narcissistic propensities. In saying this, I am speaking about narcissism writ large, about individuals with many narcissistic traits in their personalities. I am not—repeat not—saying that these political figures are suffering from NPD.

We have all heard the stories of politicians behaving poorly and often acting hypocritically. There are political scandals, fervent denials, public apologies, impeachment trials, and more. To name just a few:

**President Richard Nixon** was involved in covering up authorizing the burglary of the Democratic National Headquarters at the Watergate—but leaving a paper trail and tape-recording his meetings about it.

**President Bill Clinton** engaged in an affair with White House intern Monica Lewinsky with the transgressions occurring in the Oval Office.

**John Edwards,** the former Senator from North Carolina, who was a vice presidential nominee and a presidential candidate, was discovered to have had an extramarital affair with a woman with whom he had a child while his wife was dying of cancer. He said his infamous transgressions were due to a "narcissism that leads you to believe you can do whatever you want, you're invincible, and there will be no consequences."[133]

In 2013, Pew Research listed the forty-two most narcissistic US presidents, rating them on a scale measuring grandiose narcissism. Here are the top ten, starting with number one: Lyndon B. Johnson, Teddy Roosevelt, Andrew Jackson, Franklin D. Roosevelt, John F. Kennedy, Richard Nixon, Bill Clinton, Chester A. Arthur, Andrew Johnson, and Woodrow Wilson.[134] Of course, Donald Trump wasn't president until years later.

Because it seems that social media is a place that attracts more narcissists and narcissistic people are attracted to positions of power and leadership, what does it mean for our society if those with political power use social media for communication? Clearly, world leaders who possess traits of malignant narcissism—the dark tetrad (the dark triad plus sadism)—are the biggest worries with their access to social media and how they might use it.

One study examining the presidential election in Austria in 2016 found that narcissism, Machiavellianism, psychopathy, and everyday sadism were associated with right-wing political orientation and that psychopathy and narcissism were associated with political extremism.[135] Obviously, the more dangerous the personality traits, the more serious consequences there are for society.

I asked Agnieszka Golec de Zavala, an expert in social and personality psychology and a collective narcissism researcher, how politicians may use collective narcissists to further their own agenda, as much of her work looks at collective narcissism as it relates to prejudice, nationalism, populism, sexism, and racism. She told me:

> Because collective narcissism is about feeling that your group is *not* recognized sufficiently, political leaders can consciously capitalize on the fact that people who are collectively narcissistic will also feel entitled to action on behalf of their group. Sometimes leaders will even define their identity with a group—maybe you didn't know that your group *wasn't* recognized by others, but now you have a leader telling you so. Especially in the context where people feel undermined about their own value and feel that maybe something is wrong with them as an individual. . . but then someone tells you that it actually isn't about *you,* but about your *group.* Someone with collective narcissism will feel that they must act for the greatness of their group.

> The narcissistic narration is that: *"I can do whatever I want, and I feel relief to be whatever—sexist, racist—because it is not me. I am not a bad person because all those actions and sentiments are in the name of my group for its advancement and recognition."* This allows people to feel justified in protecting their privileges—to express racism or sexism (to name a few) because the varnish of political correctness that stopped them from expressing it before was only because societies were working on making intergroup tolerance a norm. But this is not working anymore.

Golec de Zavala believes we have abandoned the norm of inter-group tolerance and collective narcissism is a driver in the abandonment of that norm.

Golec de Zavala also told me that leaders have been doing this for centuries and that it has been proven what this rhetoric leads to when a leader capitalizes on mobilizing people for their agenda by using narcissistic narration. When you have more responsible leaders, they know what the consequences may be, but when you have less responsible leaders who want power no matter what, using this language and manipulation is an easy way to get it.

W. Keith Campbell elaborated on Golec de Zavala's concerns about narcissistic (or psychopathic) politicians online, telling me:

> The most toxic combination is a narcissistic leader with a group of followers who are a bunch of nice, agreeable people. They want to work together as a team and narcissists need a group of cohesive people. Psychopathic leaders can take over nice and compliant people. If the narrative in a war becomes, *"We can work together for each other"* it becomes a really dangerous force. So, for me, the risk is the most dangerous when narcissism is at the top. The ego ideal in the followers gets projected on the group leader (Hitler, for example) and when you do that projection, then that person becomes idealized. Then you have people getting their esteem needs met by following this narcissistic leader and it's very, very dangerous.

The advent of social media offered politicians a way to get their messaging to their audience in an unfiltered way, which was unprecedented. Prior to this, aides carefully crafted statements and speeches—which they still do—but social media offered politicians an avenue for direct, real-time messaging. With this ability comes great responsibility, and the higher up the power ladder, the louder and more powerful the messaging. An inflammatory post written by a politician is like a flamethrower.

At its best, journalism is ethical, accurate, fair, factual, and strives to pursue the truth whenever possible. However, the stratification that first came with cable news began to muddy the waters; no longer were journalists obligated to tell an opposing viewpoint if they were covering a story. The devolution continued and exploded with platforms like Twitter, which made everyone with an opinion or an axe to grind feel like a journalist. So many politicians are using social media to communicate thoughts, policies, or opinions, that the waters have gotten murkier when trying to parse out fact from fiction. Without the fact-checking and editorial review of responsible journalists, misinformation from politicians and leaders in positions of power not only contributes to an information breakdown but erodes trust and sows confusion. Social media is now like the Wild West when it comes to misinformation, the distortion of facts, and mass confusion over what is real and what is fake.

Politicians and leaders with narcissistic traits use social media for self-serving purposes and don't care what the impact is on others because their concern is only on themselves, their image, and saying whatever is necessary to stay in power. If they are severely narcissistic, social media is the ultimate form of narcissistic supply, fueling an addiction entirely concentrated on attention-seeking rather than on communicating and disseminating ideas.

The good news here is, social media can also disrupt false narratives that politicians may use to their political advantage. Politicians are often called out on their hypocrisy with "receipts" (online evidence of their hypocrisy or inauthenticity, such as former tweets) and are also held accountable in ways that were never possible before a searchable "paper" trail. Because narcissistic people (and especially the power-seeking ones) are very attracted to social media, it has also become easier to spot which politicians may be more narcissistic and what their true priorities really are. In fact, social media has highlighted phony pandering while campaigning and has given constituents a new way to call out and challenge politicians who may have let power go a little too much to their heads.

When it comes to groupthink, people can be collectively narcissistic about *any* group. Even if said group is highly revered for doing good for others, people can still have narcissistic narration around that. Think about the communal narcissist, for example, which as you may recall has created a narrative around helping others and being trustworthy. A collective narcissist can thus certainly be narcissistic around a group that is supposedly doing good for others. They will expect and feel entitled to special privileges for being so "good" or "humanitarian."

Golec de Zavala told me that unlike collective narcissists, there are also people with constructive identification with their groups. For example, one can have a sense of patriotism and feel devoted and loyal to their country or homeland, while also not exaggerating their importance. Patriotism can exist with tolerance for other groups, solidarity with other groups, and support for disadvantaged groups.

We can have healthy pride in whichever group we feel we belong to without it turning narcissistic. We can find anything we seek out on social media because every type of thought or opinion is easily found through a search function. The more we expose ourselves to the same type of narration, the more it confirms our biases that we already hold. If the exposure we get on social media is narcissistic narration, gradually that may have a negative impact on us because the more we are exposed to a consistent narration, the more likely we will be to believe it. Being open to the idea that your group is not better than or entitled to more special privileges than other groups regardless of race, ethnicity, class, gender, sexual orientation, and the like is the first step in combatting collectively narcissistic beliefs.

By understanding how narcissistic leaders may use social media to manipulate people and distort reality, my hope is that people will be able to better identify when something is said or done on social media with ill intention, especially if it presents clear danger for innocent people. No political leader is beyond reproach, and no matter what "side" someone may identify with, it's important not to blindly follow *anyone,* especially someone who may be highly narcissistic and not looking out for the good of the people.

# THE EVERYDAY POLITICAL NARCISSIST ON SOCIAL MEDIA

## Jasmine: Digital Political Power Player

Jasmine considered herself a digital political activist. Organizing and being privy to a relatively large online audience made her feel powerful and influential. Yet even in her own group, she became divisive and self-serving. Behind the scenes of the social media facade, she was often involved in power struggles with other people in her movement. Jasmine would use her flying monkeys (those who flock to narcissistic types to do their bidding) to go after anyone who she felt was a threat to her. Even a probing question on Twitter would send her on a mission to recruit others to harass and pile on that person who questioned her.

Being a celebrated activist was never really enough for her. The adoration of her online followers made her feel morally superior and above everyone else. She was someone people looked up to and went to for guidance. Jasmine was addicted to Twitter and even enjoyed hostile interactions with people under the guise of fighting for her cause. It did not matter what kind of attention she had—she wanted all of it. The more famous the person she would spar with on Twitter was, the more grandiose she felt.

People would be shocked to discover that, despite her apparent passion for those less fortunate, Jasmine did not really care about the important causes she claimed to champion. Equality, poverty, and social justice took a back seat to getting attention and power. In fact, even though Jasmine's whole persona revolved around what she believed was helping others and fighting for a better world, she was an incredibly cruel person underneath it all. One only needed to see how she treated the real people in her life. She was emotionally abusive to her friends and family and if they did not do what she asked and meet her obscenely high expectations, she would turn on them. Jasmine's behavior ran hot and cold, and people who were forced to deal with her felt like they were always walking on eggshells. To have any kind of relationship with her meant you had to read her mind and anticipate her needs or otherwise face her wrath.

When Jasmine decided to turn on the charm, however, she made you feel like the most important person in the world. She'd heap on the praise and flattery. "I don't know where I would be without you. You are so special to me." But, when she decided you had not met her unrealistic needs, she would devalue and even discard you, like you never mattered to her. "I'm sorry, but you just don't have what it takes to be here. We want the best and the brightest, and the fact that you didn't understand what I needed underscores that you are neither. It's okay to set your expectations lower, just please do it somewhere else." When her warmth shone on you, it was bright and beautiful, but when she took it away, all you would feel was icy coldness. And she made it seem as though everyone else agreed with her.

Jasmine only cared about surrounding herself with people with political influence or large social media followings. She had an over-inflated sense of self-importance and believed that her leadership was essential to the success of whatever movement she decided to lead. She truly believed that she was the center, the focus, and used a false sense of humility to act like everything she did was for the cause. She was a martyr, after all, and would never quit social media because she felt it was her duty to continue to be a leader and an activist. The reality was she could never leave social media because she was too addicted to the attention: the good, the bad, and the ugly.

## POLITICAL NARCISSISM HAS NO PARTY AFFILIATION

Political narcissism is not confined to one political party. Right before the 2016 US presidential election, a team of researchers wanted to know how narcissism related to political ideology. Interestingly, their study[136] found that there is an equal amount of narcissism with *both* the left and right political ideologies. Exhibitionism was more common with liberals (including political identification), and entitlement was more common with conservatives. Grandiose entitlement and people with exhibitionist tendencies tend to post more on social media and make their opinions known. It is quite easy to spot both entitlement and exhibitionism online, and identifying those posts gives a little window into someone's personality.

There's also evidence that specific aspects of narcissism are related to support for right-wing populist movements. One study in the *European Journal of Personality*[137] looked at far-right political parties in Germany and found that the traits of grandiose narcissism and narcissistic rivalry (characterized by aggressiveness and superiority) play a role in support for far-right political parties, and someone with the narcissistic rivalry trait will tend to agree with the statement "Other people are worth nothing."[138]

The darker, more hateful, aggressive, and dangerous aspects of narcissism might be displayed online as support for far-right parties, with social media rhetoric expressing support for these ideologies. Other research[139] suggests that those with dark tetrad traits (psychopathy, narcissism, Machiavellianism, and sadism) are more likely to believe conspiracy theories, and this is based on distrust, fatalism, odd beliefs, and desire for control.[140] Those who possess dark tetrad traits are not only more likely to believe conspiracy theories, but they will also likely perpetuate them and widely disseminate them online.

In certain instances, social media could be used to help the people who fall into misleading conspiracy theories who are not dark tetrad types. Message boards exist that are dedicated to the recovery of conspiracy followers. Those who seek help here are offered a supportive environment and will also find information that debunks the conspiracy theories. This is one way social media can be used to counter dangerous misinformation.

## COLLECTIVE NARCISSISM, RACISM, MISOGYNY, AND WHITE SUPREMACY

## Henry: Anonymous Hate Poster

Henry was a successful businessman at the top of his field but with very dark secrets. He had a vicious hobby of *anonymously* posting horrific, racist, antisemitic, Islamophobic, and misogynistic remarks online. His comments were despicable and hateful, and he would troll others and post hundreds of times a day. He managed to keep his views quiet at work but unleashed his grotesque and dangerous views online whenever he got a chance.

Henry had alias Twitter accounts and would also post on anonymous message boards. Not only did Henry find a place online to dump his secret inner thoughts, but it was also a place where he became encouraged and emboldened. The more attention and goading he received from others, the more pride he felt in himself.

None of the heinous posts or tweets need to be repeated or given any attention, but those who knew Henry were shocked to hear he was capable of such ugliness once his proclivity for hate speech came to light. (Some Internet users discovered his identity because, at some point during his incessant posting, he let some identifying information slip. The contrast between the hate he spewed online, and his public persona was so shocking, word inevitably got out.) He was once considered a respectable man in the community: married with children, successful, well-educated and with graduate degrees. He did not seem like the angry basement troll many might associate with this type of behavior.

Henry was entitled, arrogant, and had a strong need to feel superior to everyone around him. Behind closed doors, he was emotionally abusive to his wife and children, constantly putting them down and mocking them. He didn't have empathy for others and was cruel and critical at home and even sometimes at work.

Once his online aliases and racist ranting was discovered, he had to resign from his job and was socially exiled in his community.

While Henry was a lone wolf and had his own thoughts and opinions, others discover and cultivate their hateful beliefs because of what they see on online forums. A woman identified as Claire found her violent and white supremacist online beliefs through one of these forums. Speaking to *The Current* (a digital publication of Google's *Jigsaw*) she described being indoctrinated into white supremacy online, but more importantly, she discussed how she eventually found her way out of the depths of her hateful ideology.[141]

Claire had been using social media to glorify the 2019 Christchurch Mosque shootings in New Zealand where fifty-one Muslims were killed and forty were injured when she received a message from a woman who was deeply disturbed by Claire's celebration of a man who murdered innocent people based on their religion.

The woman messaging Claire, a photographer, personally knew people in the attack. She started to send Claire pictures of Muslims going about their everyday life: the images depicted them at coffee shops or hanging out with friends. The photos were the first thing that humanized Muslims to Claire. Before, all she had been exposed to in her small town and online community was blame and hatred toward Muslims.

Eventually, online interactions transitioned to phone calls, and a friendship between Claire and the photographer began to grow. Claire's racism toward Muslims began to dissipate.

While the story of Claire has a more hopeful ending, there are still many more people who continue to spread hate, indoctrinate others, and even commit or incite violent acts themselves.

While high levels of individual narcissism are linked to racism (as are Machiavellianism and psychopathy),[142] and those people are more likely to adopt right-wing authoritarian views and social dominance-oriented attitudes,[143] collective narcissism may also explain the underlying personality traits of groups who engage in online racism, or what is also referred to as "cyber racism," a term introduced by Les Back in 2002.[144]

The worry about the rise of collective narcissism simply requires revisiting recent history. As stated in the *Journal of Advances in Political Psychology* (February 2019):

> Legitimization of collective narcissism inspired not only populism and xenophobia but also atrocities committed in the name of one group against others. For example, Germans under the Nazi regime believed the superiority of their ingroup and its entitlement to a better living space was not properly appreciated by others.[145]

The same article found links between collective narcissism, authoritarianism, and social dominance-orientation (support of social hierarchies with a need for superiority). Individual narcissism and collective narcissism both revolve around feeling entitled to special privileges, which of course makes sense because unhealthy narcissism is essentially about hierarchies that create inequality.

For someone to support inequality or systems that perpetuate inequality, one has to remove themselves from the humanity of others. The reality is, until we see humans equally and deserving of the same rights and freedoms without exception, then narcissism will win. Whether it is conscious or not, narcissism is the underlying belief that *I* am more important than others, and *I* am entitled to human rights that others are not.

It goes without saying that collective and individual narcissists who may be drawn to racist, white supremacist groups online are extremely dangerous for society. Online spaces have made it much easier for hate groups such as these to indoctrinate and recruit. They don't need to pass out flyers or do face-to-face enlistment; with the Internet, there are no global boundaries, and people anywhere in the world can be reached.

The recruitment strategies are also becoming more sophisticated. *The Current's* report on violent white supremacy (cited above on the Christchurch Mosque shootings) says that radicalization thrives openly on the Internet today:

> The white supremacist movement has looser, more distributed networks than many other extremist movements. They create redundancies in their networks and decentralize their efforts to build resilience against expulsion from any individual platform. They move fluidly between mainstream and fringe platforms and use a network of services in tandem to achieve their goals. Understanding these dynamics will help us to effectively use technology to both prevent radicalization and disrupt violent movements.

While many of us might feel we are savvy enough to avoid falling into these traps, the insidious nature of these recruitment movements online may be tricker than one would think. Joanna Schroeder, a mother of young boys, shared with NPR that she was worried when she started looking at the content on Instagram's "Explore" page and saw a plethora of memes and content with racist, sexist, homophobic, and antisemitic jokes. Schroeder believes that this content is designed to radicalize young boys.[146]

While hateful content can be disguised in humor, Schroeder points out that these memes take aim at political correctness, saying things like "You can't say anything anymore" or "You're too sensitive." These statements are nothing more than gaslighting. It sends the message that mocking others is acceptable and you are overly reactive if you are offended or worried about anything that perpetuates hurtful or dangerous stereotypes about you, your identity, or any aspect of yourself. Gaslighting sends another message that it is okay to freely harm and hurt others with no accountability.

While content that depicts stereotypes may seem harmless to some, it contributes to a culture of narcissism, racism, and sexism. Younger people are rabidly consuming this content because they are inundated with it. If we can make fun of others online or use humor to disguise racist, homophobic, or misogynistic content, we are saying that a lack of empathy is okay. We are saying it is okay to be unbothered and dismissive about another person's experience in the world. It's giving a pass to feel entitled to hurt others with zero consequence.

Besides the spreading of hate in unprecedented ways because of the Internet and social media, African-American, Latinx, Asian-American, and biracial youth have reported increased racial discrimination over time in online settings.[147] In one study, African-American students in grades six through twelve were asked to describe the worst online experiences, and some of their responses included the following:

- "The worst thing that has happened to me on the Internet is that someone threatened to kill me because of my race."

- "Almost every day on Call of Duty: Black Ops (a video game) I see Confederate flags, swastikas and Black people hanging from trees in emblems and they say racist things about me and my teammates."

Journalists have also been the target of dangerous hate speech in recent years. In an article about journalists quitting Twitter,[148] many of them cited dealing with abusive behavior that they did not sign up for. Journalists facing the abuse are largely women and specifically Black or Latinx women, people of color, and LGBTQ identifying individuals. The article stated:

- A 2018 Amnesty International report[149] found that 7.1 percent of tweets sent to more than 750 study participants (female journalists and politicians based in the US and the UK) were "problematic" or "abusive"—and those numbers were much higher for Black and Latinx women than for White women.

- Several trans journalists faced online abuse and threats of violence after they tweeted criticism of an open letter decrying "cancel culture" that was signed by several prominent people with a history of anti-trans rhetoric.

These are just a few of many examples of abuse people on Twitter face simply for doing their jobs.

With both individual and collective narcissism on social media, the problem is not just contained to racist rhetoric freely shared on all corners of the web or that people can become more easily radicalized because of the vast reach of social media and the Internet. It's also possible that social media can be enhancing or even creating racism and narcissism simply by the constant exposure to information.

Golec de Zavala believes that social media could create collective narcissism, and she described an experiment to me called the "autokinetic effect." When you are in complete darkness and you see a point of light that is not moving, you have the illusion that it is moving because of the micromovements of your eyeballs. How much the illusion of the light moving is individual for each person. This gets even more interesting when you bring other people's experiences to the table. When you ask a group how much they estimate the light to move, they usually come to agree on an estimate together, and usually it is around the mean of the individual estimates. Then, they take the agreed group estimate and hold on to it as "true" or "real" because it was obtained in agreement with others. We take others as a source of information for understanding our own reality. With social media, if you look, you can find anything you want, and when you find people with whom you agree, who justify and validate your point of view, it then feels more like truth for you. This is not because you obtained evidence, but because you were validated by others sharing your opinion.

## CULTURAL NARCISSISM, SURVEILLANCE CAPITALISM, AND BIG TECH

What if the social media—narcissism problem is not just about individual narcissists or collective narcissists? The issue is bigger than all of this, and it is cultural and systemic. People have been ringing the alarms about big tech (mainly Google, Apple, Microsoft, Facebook, and Amazon) for years. What may have started out as a seed of an idea and an innovative way to connect people has now morphed into a beast that is way too powerful and exploitative to tame. These companies are part of a larger, systemic problem called "surveillance capitalism."

Coined in 2014 by Shoshanna Zuboff, a professor at Harvard Business School and author of *The Age of Surveillance Capitalism: The Fight for a Human Future at the New Frontier of Power*,[150] "surveillance capitalism" is:

> A market driven process where the commodity for sale is your personal data, and the capture and production of this data relies on mass surveillance of the Internet. This activity is often carried out by companies that provide us with free online services, such as search engines (Google) and social media platforms (Facebook).

> These companies collect and scrutinize our online behaviors (likes, dislikes, searches, social networks, purchases) to produce data that can be further used for commercial purposes. And it is often done without us understanding the full extent of the surveillance.[151]

Surveillance capitalism exploits people by mining data and using it for profit. There is an assumption that these companies are entitled to use this data without consequence, with the sole purpose of making obscene amounts of money. The abuse of power by big tech seems highly unethical, bred from a culture of narcissism. The elevation of big tech has been so alarming that it has even prompted several people from the big tech world to speak out in the extremely popular *Netflix* documentary *The Social Dilemma*.

The narcissism and abusive unchecked power intertwined with surveillance capitalism is eloquently stated by Zuboff when she says:

> Surveillance capitalism is a novel economic mutation bred from the clandestine coupling of the vast powers of the digital with the radical indifference and intrinsic narcissism of the financial capitalism and its neoliberal vision that have dominated commerce for at least three decades, especially in the Anglo economies. It is an unprecedented market form that roots and flourishes in lawless space.[152]

Surveillance capitalism is essentially a product of narcissistic culture, commanded by oligarchs who are largely submerged in their own bubbles and indifferent to the suffering of the people they believe are beneath them.

Anne Manne, social philosopher and author of several books, including of *The Life of I: The New Culture of Narcissism,* gave me her opinion on the problem, saying:

> It's about delivering people to advertisers, so there is a form of surveillance where you're looking at underwear on the Internet, and all the sudden there are underwear ads popping up on Facebook. Neoliberalism creates narcissism, but it also depends upon it because the more people are narcissistic, consumerist, materialistic, and buy more, the whole engine of capitalism thrives. This form of capitalism has found a way of reproducing itself. It is a system that is unjust, unequal, cruel, imperialist, colonialist, and it reproduces itself by creating in the psyche a kind of narcissism that is susceptible to these platforms, which then deliver those narcissistic people to the engine of capitalism, and essentially makes money out of them. There's a human side of social media, but there is also a capitalist side. People aren't subjects on Instagram or Twitter; they are objects to be used for profit.

While some companies have acknowledged and made efforts to try to stop the spread of hate, violence, and misinformation, they have also behaved unethically in censorship of the oppressed, Black indigenous and People of Color (BIPOC), all other people of color (POC), and the vulnerable. I call this phenomenon "big tech narcissism" (the exploitation, abuse of power, entitlement, and low empathy for human beings).

In *Forbes,* Janice Gassam Asare writes about how big tech silences and censors the voices of Black social media users, writing:

> Social media could use more protections and safeguards for those who are outspoken about racism and white supremacy. Black social media users have experienced a great deal of censorship online. Oftentimes, those who are outspoken about white supremacy and racism have found their content removed or taken down for violating community guidelines. The silencing of those who speak out against bigotry and hate causes more damage than harm. The dismantling of oppressive systems cannot be achieved without the hard truths. A large part of the reason why racism is such a difficult elephant to eat is because we refuse to have honest and candid conversations in person and online. But those who are courageous enough to discuss these more challenging and nuanced subjects are punished rather than praised.[153]

There are many more examples of how social media platforms are suppressing and even hiding content from people trying to show the realities of their oppression and dehumanization.

Mariam Barghouti, a Palestinian journalist, was temporarily removed from Twitter for allegedly violating their policies when she was simply reporting on the escalating violence against Palestinians during the Save Sheikh Jarrah movement in 2021. Her Twitter account was eventually restored after outrage from the Twitter community, and the company eventually apologized for the incident, saying her removal from the platform was a mistake.

Barghouti later tweeted on May 17, 2021: "I know so many Palestinian journalists, myself included, that gave up on reporting and working with news agencies because of how censored we were. The editors were so afraid that a Palestinian reporting the violence would threaten their positions. They constantly abandoned us."[154]

Social media has been entirely banned in certain countries out of fear of a political uprising. In 2016, Vietnam blocked its citizens from accessing Facebook when President Obama visited the country because they wanted to silence human rights activists.[155]

While big tech has a censorship problem and struggles with how far they should go, this example of social media being completely banned from people highlights the way social media can be used for truth—if people are allowed to use it in the first place.

The evolution of cell phones giving everyone access to a camera in their pocket has allowed people to accurately and instantaneously document some of the worst human rights violations. People can now see for themselves what is really happening in certain situations—without a filtered and biased narrative spin from corporate-owned media that is often slanted in one direction and controlled by special interests.

While video footage cannot always accurately capture the entire context of a situation, human beings have an inherent sense to know when they see something morally wrong, especially if it's violent and degrading of another person's humanity. For example, we know watching other human beings in defenseless positions get injured, brutalized, and murdered is wrong and unjustified.

The murder of George Floyd by police officer Derek Chauvin is one of the most well-known examples of a cell phone video gone viral that not only exposed truths of deep, systemic racism and police brutality but also ignited mass protests around the world. This is the aspect of social media that wields the power to portray truth in a way that is vastly different than if a journalist wrote about it, edited it, and filtered it for public consumption. Even if the truth was accurately reported, there is still no substitute for watching injustice happen in front of your eyes.

I often wonder how social media would have shaped some of the worst stains on American history had it existed at those points in time. When the US invaded Iraq in 2003, it was coincidentally the same year that MySpace and LinkedIn officially launched to the public. The initial Facebook model was not launched until 2004, and YouTube came into existence in 2005, then followed by the official launches of Facebook as we know it today, and Twitter in 2006.

The Iraq War, one of the most egregious human rights violations in recent history, was fueled by propaganda and lies to legitimize the invasion of a country following the horrific events of 9/11 by saying, erroneously, that the country was stockpiling weapons of mass destruction. It was a rush to judgment that would ultimately kill an estimated hundreds of thousands of innocent Iraqi civilians and tens of thousands of troops in the military and unleash further instability in the country and region.

The architecture of that war was a real-life horror show of dark triad traits in action and is the perfect example of narcissistic abuse of power. To justify something like an unnecessary war, you must reduce innocent people to abstractions, essentially seeing them as subhuman. The term "collateral damage" to indicate the death of civilians is the epitome of entitlement, exploitation, and a lack of empathy.

There were a few politicians who questioned going to war and stood against it, but even the left-leaning *New York Times* was supportive of the invasion. Later, in 2004, the editorial board of the esteemed newspaper issued a public apology to their readers, stating that they were misled about the weapons of mass destruction that was the so-called reason behind the war, admitting that "Editors at several levels who should have been challenging reporters and pressing for more skepticism were perhaps too intent on rushing scoops into the paper."[156]

As I think about how people were misled by political leaders and by newspapers and news outlets, I know there was a huge responsibility on all of them that they failed to meet. This is the dangerous culture of narcissism; it's the inability to understand the consequences of devastating and destructive actions.

How would social media have handled something like this? Would Facebook and Instagram have censored posts from Iraqis or people who dissented against the war? Would people have resisted or organized more with anti-war efforts and protests if they'd had the tools social media provides today?

W. Keith Campbell has considered this question, and he believes that social media might have prevented the war. He told me:

> My opinion is that social media derailed journalism completely about four to five years ago. If we had social media during the Iraq war, it wouldn't have happened because you would have had a lot of contrarian narratives out there, so they couldn't control the narrative like they did. When the government lost its monopoly on controlling the narrative through corporate media, things broke. Now they are trying to put the pieces back by controlling social media by kicking people off social media or censoring certain things. Now it's a war between centralization and decentralization of control, because the people in power want to control the narrative, and every empire wants to control the narrative.

While social media has been a force for social change, it has also evolved into a machine of disinformation. Would it have humanized Iraqis in the eyes of Americans still stung by the terrorist events of 9/11? Possibly, but, as we have seen, it is also possible to spin a completely false narrative designed to promote hatred, prejudice, racism, and violence. The bottom line is that people are in control, so it depends on who is behind the camera and the keyboard. The responsibility for truth and truth-seeking is higher than it has ever been because of the explosive growth of social media. The stakes are too high now, and we all have an obligation to try to separate fact from fiction wherever possible, and to stand up for people throughout the world who are subjected to all kinds of harm when we know in the depths of our souls that what is happening to them is wrong.

At the end of the day, narcissism is really just toxic individualism—the idea that one deserves and is entitled to more than others and that they can do whatever they want, even if it causes harm to others. Anne Manne, social philosopher and author of *The Life of I: The New Culture of Narcissism says:*

> Independence is not the ideal. There are parts of your life where you're dependent, as a child, an old person, or a sick person, and so the actual model should be *interdependence,* not selfish individualism where you don't have to look after or care for anyone else.

Terra Kater, the nurse who was cyberbullied, trolled, and doxxed for trying to counter COVID vaccine disinformation online, believes that big tech and social media are responsible for the divisiveness, misinformation, and hatred that are rampant in society now, telling me:

> I think that social media is absolutely responsible for the issues we are seeing today. Many radicalized people are now living in an entirely

different reality, and social media is to blame. I do think that the companies need to be held accountable to do more to control the amount of misinformation on their platforms. It is killing people.

It seems obvious that with everything we have come to know about how social media companies operate, they have no real investment in protecting people or in the betterment of society. Again, this book is not a place for me to stand on my soapbox and tell people what they should do with their lives both online and offline, and I believe social media is here to stay. However, given that the social media beast is largely going to go unchecked for the foreseeable future, how can people use social media in a way that is in opposition to all the insidiousness that is at the heart of big tech?

We can use social media for the collective good if we choose to, but we must be incredibly intentional in how we use it. If the best aspect of online platforms allows us to connect people all over the world, we should take that intention and use it to grow our empathy for others, help mobilize movements for justice, amplify marginalized voices, and support those who are subjugated by narcissistic systems of white supremacy.

Thinking about how we might use social media to mobilize movements for justice, fairness, and equality is a good place to start. As we've documented, misinformation and hate in the hands of narcissistic people can easily spiral out of control, so it's important to understand that not only should we not feed the trolls, we also should think twice before engaging with racist or harmful content because algorithms could increase the engagement of these posts.

How does this work? A recent study found that "out-group" animosity is a driver of engagement on social media.[157] Posts about a political out-group (the group that one does not identify with) are way more likely to be shared, driving engagement. The study also found that out-group negativity was stronger than in-group positivity, showing that divisive and angry content is more likely to go viral. Additionally, the study showed that posts about political opponents are more likely to be shared as well.

Given that humans have a propensity toward attacking an out-group and using social media to share negativity, it may be helpful to disengage from harmful content. It may also be wise to report something that is inflammatory and dangerous. However, if a narcissist is posting something antagonistic with the intention of the post going viral, the best thing to do is to not give it any attention.

When it comes to politics, racism, and prejudice, social media brings out narcissistic tendencies by constantly exposing users to echo chambers, information that has no basis in fact, a deluge of incendiary opinions, simply because many are seeking to confirm what they already believe. Social media and power-hungry politicians can use the longing to identify with a group and, for some who long to feel superior because of their own feelings of inadequacy and inferiority, to increase individual and collective narcissism.

Political Twitter is perhaps one of the most divisive and narcissistic social media forums because it truly creates animosity, a lack of empathy, and entitlement. Knowing that social media has the power to deplete some of our empathy for others and disseminate narcissistic hatred and racism, we need to understand that the addictive nature of social media should not hold so much power over how we think and see the world. If you choose to stay on social media and remain actively engaged, you now have the power to decide if you will let social media make you more or less narcissistic. My hope is that you will always choose empathy over narcissism, both in your real life and your online life.

## TIPS, TAKEAWAYS, AND FOOD FOR THOUGHT

1. Are there any political leaders or people in positions of power that influence your thinking and ideas? Do you blindly follow a politician or leader and never question them? Part of holding narcissistic people accountable, especially those in power, is questioning them and holding their feet to the fire when they (either intentionally or unintentionally) do harm to others. There is not one human on this Earth who should be blindly and completely idolized. Holding people accountable and lessening the effects of their narcissism means not treating anyone like they do no wrong. How do you hold others accountable when they should be doing better?

2. If you don't post about injustice, inequality, anti-racism, anti-sexism, and social/racial justice issues, why not? Is it fear-based? Are you conflict-avoidant? In what ways might you use social media to promote justice, and if you are white and/or privileged, how might you support your Black, Indigenous, Native American, Asian, Muslim, Arab, Jewish, Hispanic, Latinx, the disabled community, and LGBTQ friends on social media?

3. Do you follow social media accounts that shed light on injustice, important social and human rights issues, and human rights crises all over the world? Why or why not?

# Chapter 9

# USING SOCIAL MEDIA MINDFULLY: PROTECTING YOURSELF AND YOUR PEACE AND BEING AN EMPATHETIC DIGITAL CITIZEN

With all the selfie takers, poseurs, trolls, and keyboard cowboys, social media can often feel like a cesspool of narcissism. The ability to remain anonymous on the Internet and the inability to hear people's voices or see them face-to-face (unless on video) can make us lose sight of the humanity of those we interact with over screens. It is easy for someone low in empathy to feel emboldened enough to spew nonsense on the Internet, but very few people who make hateful comments online actually identify themselves. Online spaces where you don't have to identify yourself are playgrounds for narcissistic people to act out with no consequence. I will never forget reading an anonymous user's comment on a news article while researching this book that read (in reference to the pandemic): "I don't care about sacrificing for the elderly and the vulnerable. I will do what I want."

This remark was astonishingly callous, yet also somewhat misguided. The comment was probably even more disturbing to me because it was personal for me. Not only have I tried very hard to make sure my elderly parents were protected during this pandemic, but my extended family has a child cancer survivor with a very weakened immune system. I have seen her parents go through hell, dealing first with the uncertainty of her diagnosis, to then having to navigate a pandemic that could easily kill their daughter due to her severely compromised lungs from a transplant and years of cancer treatments.

As I write this, around 900,000 Americans and over 5.7 million people worldwide have died from COVID-19. These deaths are not just among elderly and immunocompromised people. In fact, I knew several healthy people in their thirties and forties who died from this disease, and all of them left behind young children, one as young as five months old. At this time, more than 140,000 children in the US have lost a primary or secondary caregiver to COVID, and this is unacceptable.

Healthcare workers have been pushed to the brink, many who have PTSD not only from witnessing tremendous amounts of pain and suffering, but also from being pushed to their limits with no breaks because of a medical system that is stretched way too thin. In fact, there are healthcare workers who have been so traumatized from all this that several have tragically killed themselves. Healthcare workers have begged unvaccinated people to care about how their actions have an impact on others. Hospitals that do not have enough resources or staff to give proper care have had to delay important care, such as surgeries and cancer treatments. When I asked nurse practitioner Terra Kater how healthcare workers are faring now, two years into the pandemic, she told me:

> In my opinion it is comparable to going through war. The amount of death and devastation we have been through has given many of us post-traumatic stress disorder (PTSD), depression, anxiety, burnout. Many have chosen to leave the profession. It has been hard to take care of people that have fallen to conspiracies. The amount of cognitive dissonance and divide is beyond draining.

Looking out for other people during a pandemic doesn't mean that everyone should hunker down in their basements and not live their lives, especially now that several years into the pandemic we know a lot more about what to do to prevent many instances of severe illness and death. Risk tolerance is different for everyone, and you can still do things in life that are enjoyable, but you can do that without abandoning decency and respect for others. However, social media has given people a platform to say whatever they want, without repercussions, and sometimes saying whatever you want leads to dangerous misinformation. For example, recall Lily, the wellness influencer from an earlier chapter, who believed in natural healing and advised cancer patients not to do chemo or radiation.

The entitled attitude of "I don't have to care about anyone else" that one encounters more often online than in real life sometimes leaves me feeling a sense of hopelessness about the fact that I'm raising my children in a world where people think, feel, and treat others as if they are disposable. So much for the campaign "We're all in this together."

The idea that "I don't have to care about others" truly sums up toxic individualism and shows a serious lack of empathy. This is one area where I really feel the impact of how toxic social media narcissism can be. If I'm scrolling through comments made by people who take their own pain out on others by throwing it into the Wild West on the Internet, my mental health is negatively impacted, and the way I begin to see other people becomes skewed. I begin to see other people as selfish and cruel instead of kind and empathetic. If you give people anonymity, a device, and Internet access, you will be sure to encounter a more unfiltered, insensitive, and dark world than you would experience in person.

True empathy means understanding that you may never have the same experience as another person, but you can still try to put yourselves in their shoes and act with compassion. We may think bad things won't happen to us and some people may believe they are invincible, but the truth is, no one is. Bad things happen to good people all the time and it's often completely random and nonsensical. If you live long enough, you'll learn that misfortune and bad luck happen to everyone.

When bad things come to pass, and they will at some point, we not only want, but need compassion and respect from others. If we are fortunate enough to live a long life, there will come a time when we are vulnerable and need help. If we are not willing to give compassion and respect, we are contributing to the culture of narcissism, and we are less likely to receive kindness in our time of need. Regardless, we should work on our empathy and how we show up in the world, simply because it's the right thing to do.

We need to pay serious attention to the narcissistic culture that social media is fueling. People are literally dying trying to take selfies on cliffs or performing crazy stunts or injuring others for likes on Instagram and TikTok. Body dysmorphia has become so problematic in Norway that the nation passed legislation mandating that influencers label their photos whenever an image is altered or retouched in an effort to combat insecurity around body image. Any violation to this law can result in fine or imprisonment. According to *Vice*, the Norwegian Ministry of Children and Family said, "Body pressure is always there, often imperceptibly, and is difficult to combat. A requirement for retouched or otherwise manipulated advertising to be marked is one measure against body pressure." The ministry also went on to say that "The measure will hopefully make a useful and significant contribution to curbing the negative impact that such advertising has, especially on children and young people."[158]

We in the United States should also think about strategies such as this—or anything we can do to move away from the excessive focus on materialism and image at the expense of being a citizen who contributes positively to their communities and the world. I believe the first step is to unplug as much as possible and to use social media mindfully and sparingly. While that sort of advice may seem obvious and discussed excessively, we rarely follow through because of the addictive nature of the technology. But if you can wrest yourself away from your phone or computer, you will experience less narcissism offline, where people are not going to feel free to spout their secret, entitled, arrogant, and often racist and misogynistic feelings and beliefs. If you see cruelty when you are online, and of course in person, consider doing a good deed or something kind for someone else to negate the nastiness.

W. Keith Campbell offers some prescient advice regarding this topic:

Disconnecting isn't a bad thing. People started migrating from Instagram to TikTok because there was less pressure to look good, so there has been some transition away from those more classically narcissistic sites. There is probably some awareness that this stuff is fake, but even if you know it, it still works. The Hollywood illusion still works. Just focus on having friends. If you eat well, exercise, have friends, and get outdoors, you're going to be okay. Do this to balance the toxic stuff of social media. Build a life you like, and then you don't have to worry about stuff on the outside.

Cultivate an online space for yourself that is narcissism-free. If influencer or celebrity accounts make you feel inadequate, insecure, unworthy, or even if you are just rolling your eyes at them, unfollow them. If someone's excessive posting or constant selfies give you the same reactions, unfollow or mute them. Only follow those that enhance your online experience; life is too short to expose yourself to negativity that makes you feel bad about yourself.

As in life, on social media there are people worth engaging with, and there are total lost causes—those with whom you will never have a meaningful or productive exchange. It goes without saying that you should not spend your energy on the lost causes. Do not feed the trolls, no matter how badly you might want to set them straight! You will never be able to carry on a civil dialogue with them. Beyond the obvious, how do you decide which people will be accountable when they make a mistake? As we have discussed in detail, look at their reactions to gauge what kind of person you are dealing with. Defensiveness, blame shifting, and gaslighting are all tactics of narcissistic abuse, and whether the person using them is a narcissist or not, they will make you feel angry, confused, irritated, sad, defeated, and more.

Narcissistic influencers, celebrities, spiritual gurus, bloggers, and anyone you may encounter might use narcissistic defenses if called out on something they post that is hurtful or irresponsible. If they offer an apology after being called out by many followers and social media users, it is up to you to decide if it feels genuine and authentic and if you want to continue to follow them and engage with them.

Try to think about what you say or comment on online, especially if you are doing it anonymously. You know the old saying, "If you don't have anything nice to say, don't say it at all." That may be the best policy when engaging on social media. There are ways to express yourself and share your frustration and anger without resorting to inflammatory rhetoric, name-calling, bullying, and even threats.

If someone is inflammatory and disrespectful toward you online, don't feel bad about removing them from your friend list—or your life. How someone acts behind a keyboard is also a clue to how they will treat you offline. If the relationship is important, have a conversation about the social media fallout *in person*. A back-and-forth over electronic communication when in conflict almost never goes well.

## RELATIONSHIP BOUNDARIES ON SOCIAL MEDIA

As for your relationships with your loved ones and children, think deeply about what you post and how it might impact them. Have honest conversations with your partner about what boundaries you have for yourselves and your children (if you have them) on social media. Consider who you share things with. Is sharing about your children online totally off limits, or does it make sense to have a small account with only your most trusted people on it? Remember that even with the most secure privacy settings and trusted people, there is always the possibility of losing a device or getting hacked, and that means nothing is 100 percent safe. Some people are fine with that and take a balanced approach.

Helping youth navigate social media is tougher. At what age do you give your child a smart phone, if at all? Maybe the phone is for emergency use only and doesn't have apps, or maybe parents have access to the passwords. While each parental choice will be different based on the individual child, there are many great parenting experts and therapists out there who have good guidelines and can help you tailor them to the individual child.

Many people want to believe in the inherent goodness of others, and because personality traits, both "good" and "bad," are all on spectrums, it is hard to see people as all bad. When we see the glimmers of good, even in the most toxic people, it can make it easier for us to slide back into old patterns with them, forgive them, and keep them in our lives. Especially for people with significant trauma, it can be especially difficult to identify and label toxic abuse and behavior and even harder to extricate themselves from unhealthy or abusive situations.

If someone is severely narcissistic, high on the narcissism spectrum, or NPD (including malignant and dark triad/tetrad), then the chances of them changing are quite low, if almost nonexistent. Unless the person has some insight or awareness and truly wants to change, the vicious cycle of abusive patterns and behaviors will continue, online and offline. Cutting these people off and having no contact (if you have the ability to do so) is the best policy when looking to protect yourself.

Safeguarding yourself, as well as maintaining your peace and serenity, is the top priority. *You* get to decide whom you want in your life. Many of us (especially women) are conditioned to think that having boundaries and protecting our personal space is rude. Online we may think unfriending, blocking, or muting is rude or extreme. It is no one's place but yours to decide what you should do with your friend list or your social media accounts. If you choose to have social media accounts, empower yourself to make cyberspace a healthy space for you.

## SHOULD YOU DELETE YOUR SOCIAL MEDIA ACCOUNTS?

There are many social media and digital experts out there who believe a mass exodus of social media is the only way out of the madness it has created. Jaron Lanier, known as "the father of virtual reality" and an intensely fierce advocate of deleting your social media accounts (he even wrote a book titled *Ten Arguments for Deleting Your Social Media Accounts Right Now*) has some convincing reasons why you should. He challenges many of the arguments for why social media can be good, especially when it comes to social change, political movements for freedom and equality, and general awareness of important issues. In an interview with *Recode (Vox)*, he said:

> I suggest in one of the arguments in the book, the one about politics, that oftentimes when people think they're being productive and improving society on social media, actually they're not because the part of the social media machine that's operating behind the scenes, which are the algorithms that are attempting to engage people more and more and influence them on behalf of advertisers and all of this, are turning whatever energy you put into the system into fuel to drive the system. And it often is the case that the fuel you put in is better driving the reaction than the original. The enthusiasms that drove the Arab Spring turned out to be even more efficient for introducing the

people that turned into ISIS to each other, in recruiting for them. Black Lives Matter in the US turned out to be more efficient for creating a resurgence of the KKK and Neo-Nazis that we hadn't seen in memory, you know? So, it might seem to you like you're using social media more and more effectively, but so far, the pattern is that you're wrong.[159]

Anne Manne offers a similar opinion, stating:

There are occasions where social media can arouse empathy and be a political force. The problem as I see it is that those moments are much rarer, and clever narcissists are able to manipulate followers where people are all running in unison. It's almost like the old Wild West movies and posses, where we set upon posses to pile on to someone. Because the platforms are so disgraceful, they act as a megaphone for misogyny. The classic idea of liberalism from John Stewart Mill was that you could do whatever you like and have liberty, until you harm someone else. So, the examples where social media has acted as a force for good to me would be far less than the examples of collective fury, thwarted entitlement for men, and the dark net.

It could be argued that keeping our social media accounts could be feeding into cultural narcissism—and in all honesty, social media is certainly not making any of us less narcissistic. There is good evidence to suggest that social media can gradually make us more narcissistic because, from a social psychology perspective, social media can have an impact on our behavior. It may not happen overnight, but if we are exposed to something consistently over a period of time, it can influence us. For some of us, deleting all social media accounts and becoming as private as possible is the right decision.

However, I am a realist, and I know that there will not be a mass exodus from social media anytime soon, if at all, in most our lifetimes.

In fact, the amount of people using social media increases yearly. All I can do is present information and let people make an educated decision on what they believe is best for them.

If social media is here to stay, then we should find every way possible to use it for good, and it is certainly not all bad. If narcissism, whether it is individual, collective, or cultural, is the underbelly of the darkness of social media, then the opposite of narcissism is one of the anecdotes to the ugliness that harms so many on social media and the Internet.

Therefore, if someone is celebrating something on social media, celebrate with them. If someone writes a post and it is obvious they are looking for compassion and support, give it to them. If cyberbullies can make people feel suicidal, and even push them to kill themselves, imagine if people received the opposite messages and were affirmed, supported, and given the gift of feeling seen and heard?

If you use social media as a form of activism, translate it to the real world. Social media activism can sometimes be seen as virtue signaling and hollow if there is no meaning or real-world action behind the post. As we have seen with communal narcissism, virtue signaling and posting about causes and good deeds is not necessarily done with good intention, or intention to help others. It is often done just for a boost in followers, or a boost in ego and narcissistic supply.

At the end of the day, what you do in your daily life out in the world is more important than your online life. The best way to use social media is to live most of your life interacting with others outside of electronic communication. In 2022, there is hope that many of us can abandon our devices more and live our lives with the people that mean the most to us. If anything, the global pandemic has given us all a newfound appreciation for how important in-person interactions are, and how critical they are for our mental health. Whatever you choose to do with your social media accounts, be intentional, be kind, and surround yourself with people that uplift you, on Facebook and in real life.

## TAKEAWAYS, TIPS, AND FOOD FOR THOUGHT

1. Have you ever joined a community-based organization or socially minded group after reading a social media post about it?
2. In what ways can you use social media to uplift and help others? Some examples could include: an honorary birthday or "just because" appreciation post; sending thoughtful and loving comments; uplifting someone and cheering them on when they have an accomplishment; using compassionate support when someone shares a difficult thing on social media; donating to someone's cause through social media; engaging in productive and respectful debate; sharing something of someone else's that will help them or their business.
3. What will you do to use social media more mindfully going forward? Will you delete your account, limit your use, or change the way you use social media?

# ENDNOTES

## Introduction

[1]Timo Gnambs and Markus Appel, "Narcissism and Social Networking Behavior: A Meta-Analysis," *Journal of Personality* 86, no. 2 (2017): pp. 200-212, https://doi.org/10.1111/jopy.12305.

[2]Phil Reed et al., "Visual Social Media Use Moderates the Relationship between Initial Problematic Internet Use and Later Narcissism," *The Open Psychology Journal*, accessed November 2, 2020. https://benthamopen.com/FULLTEXT/TOPSYJ-11-163.

[3]Brittany Gentile, et al., "The Effect of Social Networking Websites on Positive Self-Views: An Experimental Investigation," *Computers in Human Behavior*, September 2012. https://www.sciencedirect.com/science/article/abs/pii/S0747563212001409.

[4]Zack Friedman. "78% of Workers Live Paycheck to Paycheck." Forbes Magazine, January 11, 2019. https://www.forbes.com/sites/zackfriedman/2019/01/11/live-paycheck-to-paycheck-government-shutdown/.

[5]Pam Fessler. "U.S. Census Bureau Reports Poverty Rate Down, But Millions Still Poor." NPR, September 10, 2019. https://www.npr.org/2019/09/10/759512938/u-s-census-bureau-reports-poverty-rate-down-but-millions-still-poor.

[6]Anne Manne. *The Life of I: The New Culture of Narcissism.* Carlton, Victoria: Melbourne University Press, 2015.

[7]W. Keith Campbell with Carolyn Crist. *The New Science of Narcissism: Understanding One of the Greatest Psychological Challenges of Our Time--and What You Can Do About It.* Boulder, CO: Sounds True, 2020.

## Chapter 1

[8]Craig Malkin, *Rethinking Narcissism: The Secret to Recognizing and Coping with Narcissists* (New York: Harper Perennial, 2016).

[9]"I'm Ok, You're Not Ok." Max-Planck-Gesellschaft, October 9, 2013. https://www.mpg.de/research/supramarginal-gyrus-empathy.

[10]EXPLOITATION: Definition in the Cambridge English Dictionary," accessed June 23, 2020, https://dictionary.cambridge.org/us/dictionary/english/exploitation.

[11]"Self-Absorbed." Merriam-Webster Dictionary. Accessed June 16, 2020. https://www.merriam-webster.com/dictionary/self-absorbed.

[12]Leon F. Seltzer. "Self-Absorption: The Root of All (Psychological) Evil?" *Psychology Today.* Sussex Publishers, August 24, 2016. https://www.psychologytoday.com/us/blog/evolution-the-self/201608/self-absorption-the-root-all-psychological-evil.

[13]Monique Tello, M. D. (2018, October 16). *Trauma-informed care: What it is, and why it's important.* Harvard Health. Retrieved February 11, 2022, from https://www.health.harvard.edu/blog/trauma-informed-care-what-it-is-and-why-its-important-2018101613562

[14]"SAMHSA's Concept of Trauma and Guidance for a Trauma-Informed Approach." SAMHSA Publications and Digital Products. Accessed June 15, 2020. https://store.samhsa.gov/product/SAMHSA-s-Concept-of-Trauma-and-Guidance-for-a-Trauma-Informed-Approach/SMA14-4884.

[15]Bill Gordon, "Excessive Attention-Seeking and Drama Addiction," *Psychology Today* (Sussex Publishers, November 4, 2014). https://www.psychologytoday.com/us/blog/obesely-speaking/201411/excessive-attention-seeking-and-drama-addiction.

[16]"What Are the DSM-5 Diagnostic Criteria for Narcissistic Personality Disorder (NPD)?" Latest Medical News, Clinical Trials, Guidelines—Today on Medscape. November 10, 2019. Accessed June 21, 2020. https://www.medscape.com/answers/1519417-101764/what-are-the-dsm-5-diagnostic-criteria-for-narcissistic-personality-disorder-npd.

[17]C. Nathan DeWall, W. Keith Campbell, Buffardi Laura, and Bonser Ian. "Narcissism and Implicit Attention Seeking: Evidence from Linguistic Analyses of Social Networking and Online Presentation." Elsevier.com, March 31, 2011. http://citeseerx.ist.psu.edu/viewdoc/download?doi=10.1.1.592.6468&rep=rep1&type=pdf.

[18]P. Sorokowski, A. Sorokowska, A. Oleszkiewicz, et al. "Selfie Posting Behaviors Are Associated with Narcissism among Men," May 15, 2015. https://www.sciencedirect.com/science/article/abs/pii/S0191886915003256.

[19]Christina Shane-Simpson, Anna M. Schwartz, Rudy Abi-Habib, et al. "I Love My Selfie! An Investigation of Overt and Covert Narcissism to Understand Selfie-Posting Behaviors within Three Geographic Communities." *Computers in Human Behavior.* Pergamon, October 3, 2019. https://www.sciencedirect.com/science/article/abs/pii/S074756321930370X.

[20]Simine Vazire, Laura Paige Naumann, Peter J. Rentfrow, and Samuel D. Gosling. "Portrait of a Narcissist: Manifestations of Narcissism in Physical Appearance." *Journal of Research in Personality,* December 2008. https://doi.org/https://www.researchgate.net/publication/222511498_Portrait_of_a_narcissist_Manifestations_of_narcissism_in_physical_appearance.

[21]Berit Brogaard, "6 Signs That You Might Be a Vulnerable Narcissist," March 31, 2020., https://www.psychologytoday.com/us/blog the-superhuman-mind/202003/6-signs-you-might-be-vulnerable-narcissist.

[22]J.E. Gebauer et al., "Communal Narcissism," *Journal of Personality and Social Psychology,* accessed June 29, 2020, https://psycnet.apa.org/record/2012-21491-001.

[23]Jochen E. Gebauer et al., "Communal Narcissism Inventory," *PsycTESTS Dataset,* 2012, https://doi.org/10.1037/t21485-000.

[24]Magdalena Żemojtel-Piotrowska, Anna Z. Czarna, Jarosław Piotrowski, et al. "Structural Validity of the Communal Narcissism Inventory (CNI): The Bifactor Model." *Personality and Individual Differences.* Pergamon, November 25, 2015. https://www.sciencedirect.com/science/article/pii/S0191886915300568.

[25]Vicki S. Helgeson and Heidi L. Fritz, "A Theory of Unmitigated Communion," *Personality and Social Psychology Review 2,* no. 3 (1998): pp. 173-183. https://doi.org/10.1207/s15327957pspr0203_2.

[26]Joyce Lui, Julie Chrysosferidis, Zeinab seyed zeinab Mousavi, and Christopher Barry. "Perceptions of Agentic and Communal Narcissism on Facebook." ResearchGate, July 2019. https://www.researchgate.net/publication/334666290_Perceptions_of_Agentic_and_Communal_Narcissism_on_Facebook.

[27]Zavala, A. G. de, Dyduch-Hazar, K., & Lantos, D. (2019, March 20). *Collective narcissism: Political consequences of investing self worth in the ingroup's image.* Wiley Online Library. Retrieved February 11, 2022, from https://onlinelibrary.wiley.com/doi/full/10.1111/pops.12569

[28]Agnieszka Golec de Zavala, "Why Collective Narcissists Are So Politically Volatile," Aeon, June 30, 2020. https://aeon.co/ideas/why-collective-narcissists-are-so-politically-volatile.

[29]Agnieszka Golec de Zavala et al., "Table 1 Items of the Collective Narcissism Scale," December 19, 2017. https://www.researchgate.net/figure/tems-of-the-Collective-Narcissism-Scale-Gole.

[30]Aleksandra Cichocka, and Aleksandra Cislak. "Nationalism as Collective Narcissism." *Current Opinion in Behavioral Sciences* 34 (2020): 69–74. https://doi.org/10.1016/j.cobeha.2019.12.013.

[31]Alexandra Samet. "How the Coronavirus Is Changing US Social Media Usage." *Insider Intelligence,* July 29, 2020. https://www.emarketer.com/content/how-coronavirus-changing-us-social-media-usage.

## Chapter 2

[32]Rock, David. "Your Brain on Facebook." *Harvard Business Review,* July 23, 2014. https://hbr.org/2012/05/your-brain-on-facebook.

[33]Newsroom, UC. "Find Social Media Frustrating? Try Empathy." University of California, February 11, 2020. https://www.universityofcalifornia.edu/news/social-media-making-you-frustrated-try-empathy#:~:

[34]Jessie Sun, Kelsi Harris, and Simine Vazire. "Is Well-Being Associated with the Quantity and Quality of Social Interactions?" *Journal of Personality and Social Psychology.* U.S. National Library of Medicine. Accessed May 4, 2021. https://pubmed.ncbi.nlm.nih.gov/31647273/.

[35]Ruyle, Kim. "The Neuroscience of Reward and Threat." Main, December 8, 2017. https://www.td.org/insights/the-neuroscience-of-reward-and-threat.

[36]C. T. Barry, H. Doucette, D. C. Loflin, N. Rivera-Hudson, L. L. Herrington. "Let Me Take a Selfie": Associations between Self-Photography, Narcissism, and Self-Esteem. *Psychol. Pop. Media Cult.,* 2017 6:48 10.1037/ppm0000089

[37]L. E. Buffardi, Campbell W. K. (2008). Narcissism and Social Networking Web Sites. Pers. Soc. *Psychol. Bull.* 34 1303–1314. 10.1177/0146167208320061

[38]Kyle Nash, Andre Johansson, and Kumar Yogeeswaran. "Social Media Approval Reduces Emotional Arousal for People High in Narcissism: Electrophysiological Evidence." *Frontiers in Human Neuroscience.* Frontiers Media S.A., September 20, 2019. https://www.ncbi.nlm.nih.gov/pmc/articles/PMC6764241/#B6.

[39]Anisa Purbasari Horton, "Yes, Social Media Is Making You Miserable." *Fast Company,* October 28, 2019. https://www.fastcompany.com/90415438/yes-social-media-is-making-you-miserable.

[40]Joseph A. Shrand, MD. "Why Do We Need to Feel Valued?" *Psychology Today.* Sussex Publishers. May 18, 2021, accessed May 6, 2021. https://www.psychologytoday.com/us/blog/the-i-m-approach/202005/why-do-we-need-feel-valued.

## Chapter 3

[41]Julia Brailovskaia, Elke Rohmann, Hans-Werner Bierhoff, and Jürgen Margraf. "The Anxious Addictive Narcissist: The Relationship between Grandiose and Vulnerable Narcissism, Anxiety Symptoms and Facebook Addiction." PLOS ONE. Public Library of Science. Accessed May 6, 2021. https://journals.plos.org/plosone/article?id=10.1371%2Fjournal.pone.0241632.

[42]Panchal Nirmita, Rabah Kamal, and Feb 2021. "The Implications of COVID-19 for Mental Health and Substance Use." KFF, April 14, 2021. https://www.kff.org/coronavirus-covid-FN19/issue-brief/the-implications-of-covid-19-for-mental-health-and-substance-use/#:~:text=Older%20adults%20are%20also%20more,prior%20to%20the%20current%20crisis.

[43]FightMediocrity. "Why Is an Ordinary Life Not Good Enough Anymore? Alain De Botton." YouTube, October 4, 2020. https://www.youtube.com/watch?v=1KDB42qGT-8. "Social Media Habits: Can They Negatively Impact Mental Health?" Treated.com. Accessed March 5, 2022. https://www.treated.com/blog/social-media-habits-and-mental-health.

[44]Post, Stephen G. "Altruism, Happiness, and Health: It's Good to Be Good." *International Journal of Behavioral Medicine,* 2005. https://greatergood.berkeley.edu/images/uploads/Post-AltruismHappinessHealth.pdf.

## Chapter 4

[45]Zimmerman, M. (2022, February 8). *Overview of personality disorders—psychiatric disorders.* Merck Manuals Professional Edition. Retrieved February 11, 2022, from https://www.merckmanuals.com/professional/psychiatric-disorders/personality-disordersoverview-of-personality-disorders

[46]Swansea University, "Excessive Posting of Photos on Social Media Is Associated with Increase in Narcissism." Medical Xpress, November 9, 2018. https://medicalxpress.com/news/2018-11-excessive-photos-social-media-narcissism.html.

[47]Fakhra Jabeen, Charlotte Gerritsen, and Jan Treur. "Narcissism and Fame: A Complex Network Model for the Adaptive Interaction of Digital Narcissism and Online Popularity." Applied Network Science. Springer International Publishing, October 31, 2020. https://appliednetsci.springeropen.com/articles/10.1007/s41109-020-00319-6.

[48]Campbell, W. Keith, and Carolyn Crist. "5 Key Aspects of Social Media and Narcissism." *Psychology Today.* Sussex Publishers. Accessed May 10, 2021. https://www.psychologytoday.com/us/blog/new-science-narcissism /202010/5-key-aspects-social-media-and-narcissism.

[49]"I Was Insta-Famous and It Was One of the Worst Things to Happen in My 20s | Verity Johnson." *The Guardian,* July 18, 2019. https://www.theguardian.com/commentisfree/2019/jul/19/i-was-insta-famous-and-it-was-one-of-the-worst-things-to-happen-in-my-20s.

[50]Georgia Akande, "Awin Survey Results: British Children Aspiring to Be Social Media Influencers." *Awin,* March 20, 2020. https://www.awin.com/gb/news-and-events/awin-news/awin-survey-results-british-children-aspiring-to-be-social-media-influencers.

[51]Aphrodite Papadatou, "1 of 5 British Children Want a Career as Social Media Influencers." *HRreview,* September 12, 2019. https://www.hrreview.co.uk/hr-news/1-of-5-british-children-want-a-career-as-social-media-influencers/114597.

[52]"Have a Little Empathy': Bali Tires of Badly Behaved Foreign Influencers." *The Guardian.,* May 14, 2021. https:/www.theguardian.com/global-development/2021/may/14have-a-little-empathy-bali-tires-of-badly-behaved-foreign-influencers.

[53]Jean M. Twenge and W. Keith Campbell. *The Narcissism Epidemic: Living in the Age of Entitlement.* New York, NY: Atria Paperback, 2013.

[54]"Reality TV Stars Auditioned to 'Promote' Poison Diet Drink on Instagram." BBC News. BBC, December 18, 2019. https://www.bbc.com/news/newsbeat-50837267.

[55]Weill, Kelly. "The Absurd Get-Rich-Quick Schemes Hyped by Far-Right GOPers." The Daily Beast, February 8, 2021. https://www.thedailybeast.com/meet-the-elected-coronavirus-clowns-hyping-get-rich-quick-schemes.

[56]Eric Rosenberg, "3 Mind Blowing Statistics About MLMs." Due, October 31, 2018. https://due.com/blog/3-mind-blowing-statistics-about-mlms/#:~:text=It's%20hard%20to%20succeed%20in,39x%20better%20than%20an%20MLM.

[57]Casey Bond, "MLMs Are a Nightmare for Women and Everyone They Know." HuffPost, January 29, 2021. https://www.huffpost.com/entry/mlm-pyramid-scheme-target-women-financial-freedom_l_5d0bfd60e4b07ae90d9a6a9e.

[58]Martinez-Lewi, L. (2013, July 29). Covert Narcissists Hiding in Holiness–Yoga Divas–Spiritual Gurus [web log]. Retrieved February 10, 2022, from https://thenarcissistinyourlife.com/covert-narcissists-hiding-in-holiness-yoga-divas-spiritual-gurus/.

[59]Arabi, S. (2017, July 8). *5 signs youre dealing with a dangerous narcissistic healer or guru.* Psych Central. Retrieved February 11, 2022, from https://psychcentral.com/blog/recovering-narcissist/2017/07/5-signs-youre-dealing-with-a-dangerous-narcissistic-healer-or-guru

[60]S. Mark Young, and Drew Pinsky. "Narcissism and Celebrity." *Journal of Research in Personality.* Academic Press, June 30, 2006. https://www.sciencedirect.com/science/article/abs/pii/S0092656606000778?via%3Dihub.

[61]Stephanie Soucheray, "US Job Losses Due to COVID-19 Highest since Great Depression." CIDRAP, May 8, 2020. https://www.cidrap.umn.edu/news-perspective/2020/05/us-job-losses-due-covid-19-highest-great-depression.

[62]Spencer Kornhaber, "The Pandemic Clarified Who the Kardashians Really Are." *The Atlantic,* December 1, 2020. https://www.theatlantic.com/culture/archive/2020/11/how-covid-19-dethroned-kardashians/617125/.

[63]Jon Caramanica, "This 'Imagine' Cover Is No Heaven." *New York Times,* March 20, 2020. https://www.nytimes.com/2020/03/20/arts/music/coronavirus-gal-gadot-imagine.html.

[64]A.T. Cheng, Hawton, K., Chen, T.H., et al., "The Influence of Media Coverage of a Celebrity Suicide on Subsequent Suicide Attempts." *Journal of Clinical Psychiatry.* U.S. National Library of Medicine. Accessed May 16, 2021. https://pubmed.ncbi.nlm.nih.gov/17592909/.

[65]Ovul Sezer, Francesca Gino, and Michael Norton. "Humblebragging: A distinct—and ineffective —self-presentation strategy." *Journal of Personality and Social Psychology.* " APA PsycNet." American Psychological Association. Accessed May 20, 2021. https://psycnet.apa.org/doiLanding?doi=10.1037%2Fpspi0000108.

[66]Jamie Ducharme, "Humblebragging Makes People Dislike You, According to Science." *Time,* January 10, 2018. https://time.com/5095144/humblebrag-bragging/.

## Chapter 5

[67]Wendy Wang, "Who Cheats More? The Demographics of Infidelity in America." Institute for Family Studies, January 10, 2018. https://ifstudies.org/blog/who-cheats-more-the-demographics-of-cheating-in-america.

[68]Daniel N. Jones, and Dana A. Weiser. "Differential Infidelity Patterns among the Dark Triad." *Personality and Individual Differences.* Pergamon, September 29, 2013. https://www.sciencedirect.com/science/article/abs/pii/S0191886913012634.

[69]James K. McNulty, and Laura Widman. "Sexual Narcissism and Infidelity in Early Marriage." Archives of Sexual Behavior. U.S. National Library of Medicine, October 2014. https://www.ncbi.nlm.nih.gov/pmc/articles/PMC4163100/.

[70]Irum Saeed Abbasi, "Addiction to Social Networking Sites Linked to Romantic Disengagement and Infidelity-Related Behaviors." PsyPost, April 13, 2019. https://www.psypost.org/2019/02/addiction-to-social-networking-sites-linked-to-romantic-disengagement-and-infidelity-related-behaviors-

[71]Russell B. Clayton, Keith M. Harris and Elias Aboujaoude, et al. "The Third Wheel: The Impact of Twitter Use on Relationship Infidelity and Divorce." Mary Ann Liebert, Inc., publishers, July 3, 2014. https://www.liebertpub.com/doi/abs/10.1089/cyber.2013.0570.

[72]Angela Browne, "Online Infidelity: Gender, Narcissism and Extraversion as Predictors of Behaviour and Jealousy Responses." DBS eSource Home. Dublin Business School, January 1, 1970. https://esource.dbs.ie/handle/10788/2779.

[73]Henry M. Seiden, "Creating Passion: An Internet Love Story." *Journal of Applied Psychoanalytic Studies.* Kluwer Academic Publishers-Plenum Publishers. Accessed May 24, 2021. https://link.springer.com/article/10.1023/A:1010109627151.

[74]Ilan Aviram, and Yair Amichai-Hamburger. "Online Infidelity: Aspects of Dyadic Satisfaction, Self-Disclosure, and Narcissism." OUP Academic. Oxford University Press, July 17, 2017. https://academic.oup.com/jcmc/article/10/3/JCMC1037/4614444.

[75]Tara C. Marshall, Kathrine Bejanyan, Gaia Di Castro, and Ruth A. Lee. "Attachment Styles as Predictors of Facebook-Related Jealousy and Surveillance in Romantic Relationships." Wiley Online Library. John Wiley & Sons, Ltd, January 16, 2012. https://onlinelibrary.wiley.com/doi/abs/10.1111/j.1475-6811.2011.01393.x.

[76]Daniel Halpern, James E. Katz, and Camila Carril. "The Online Ideal Persona vs. the Jealousy Effect: Two Explanations of Why Selfies Are Associated with Lower-Quality Romantic Relationships." *Telematics and Informatics.* Pergamon, May 3, 2016. https://www.sciencedirect.com/science/article/abs/pii/S0736585316300545.

[77]"Catfishing." Wikipedia, April 23, 2021. https://en.wikipedia.org/wiki/Catfishing.

[78]Kirk Fortini, "False Online Personas: Who Creates Them and Why?" CSUSB ScholarWorks. Accessed May 21, 2021. https://scholarworks.lib.csusb.edu/meeting-minds/2015/oral-pres-full/70/.

[79]Eric Vanman, "It's Not about Money: We Asked Catfish Why They Trick People Online." The Conversation, June 4, 2019. https://theconversation.com/its-not-about-money-we-asked-catfish-why-they-trick-people-online-100381.

[80]Gavin de Becker, *The Gift of Fear: Survival Signals That Protect Us from Violence.* New York: Back Bay Books/Little, Brown and Company, 2021.

[81]Shahida Arabi, "Can You Spot a Narcissist Online? 3 Surprising Behaviors Which Reveal Predators in Cyberspace." Psych Central, October 23, 2019. https://psychcentral.com/blog/recovering-narcissist/2019/10/can-you-spot-a-narcissist-online-3-surprising-behaviors-which-reveal-predators-in-cyberspace#6.

## Chapter 6

[82]Ryan Grenoble, "Utah Mom Finds Stolen Facebook Photos of Her Kids Promoting Porn Sites." HuffPost, May 5, 2015.

[83]"Children's Online Privacy Protection Rule ('COPPA')." Federal Trade Commission, December 1, 2020. https://www.ftc.gov/enforcement/rules/rulemaking-regulatory-reform-proceedings/childrens-online-privacy-protection-rule.

[84]"Grandmother Ordered to Delete Facebook Photos under GDPR." BBC News, May 21, 2020. https://www.bbc.com/news/technology-52758787.

[85]Eva Latipah, H. Kistoro, Fitria Fauziah Hasanah, and Himawan Putranta. "[PDF] Elaborating Motive and Psychological Impact of Sharenting in Millennial Parents." *Universal Journal of Educational Research,* October 1, 2020. https://www.semanticscholar.org/paper/Elaborating-Motive-and-Psychological-Impact-of-in-Latipah-Kistoro/98b99cf-c6947115796fcabba5ad6b10aa7eab03c.

[86]Lisa Lazard, Abigail Locke, Charlotte Dann, Rose Capdevila, and Sandra Roper, "Sharenting: Why Mothers Post about Their Children on Social Media." *The Conversation,* January 22, 2021. https://theconversation.com sharenting-why-mothers-post-about-their-children-on-social-media-91954.

[87]Helier Cheung, "Can You Stop Your Parents Sharing Photos of You Online?" BBC News, March 28, 2019. https://www.bbc.com/news/world-47722427.

[88]Leah A. Plunkett, *Sharenthood: Why We Should Think before We Talk about Our Kids Online.* MIT Press, 2020.

[89]Delia Paunescu, "What to Know before Posting a Photo of Your Kids on Social Media." Vox, November 26, 2019. https://www.vox.com/recode/2019/11/26/20983980posting-kids-photos-online-privacy-sharenting-reset-podcast.

[90]Priya Kumar, "The Real Problem with Posting about Your Kids Online." *Fast Company,* February 6, 2019. https://www.fastcompany.com/90301875 the-real-problem-with-posting-about-your-kids-online.

[91]"Young Adults Distressed by Labels of Narcissism, Entitlement." *ScienceDaily,* May 15, 2019. https://www.sciencedaily.com/releases/2019/05/190515144006.htm.

[92]Niraj Chokshi, "Attention Young People: This Narcissism Study Is All About You." *New York Times,* May 15, 2019. https://www.nytimes.com/2019/05/15/science/narcissism-teen-agers.html.

[93]Gabrielle Coppola, Pasquale Musso, et al. "The Apple of Daddy's Eye: Parental Overvaluation Links the Narcissistic Traits of Father and Child." *International Journal of Environmental Research and Public Health.* MDPI, July 30, 2020. https://www.ncbi.nlm.nih.gov/pmc/articles/PMC7432641/. Brummelman, Eddie, Sander Thomaes, Stefanie A Nelemans, Bram Orobio de Castro, Geertjan Overbeek, and Brad J Bushman. "Origins of Narcissism in Children." Proceedings of the National Academy of Sciences of the United States of America. National Academy of Sciences, March 24, 2015. https://www.ncbi.nlm.nih.gov/pmc/articles/PMC4378434/.

[94]Otto F. Kernberg, Borderline Conditions and Pathological Narcissism. Lanham, Mar.: Rowman & Littlefield, 2004.

[95]Carrie James, a Katie Davis, et al. "Digital Life and Youth Well-being, Social Connectedness, Empathy, and Narcissism." American Academy of Pediatrics, November 1, 2017. https://pediatrics.aappublications.org/content/140/Supplement_2/S71.

[96]L. Mark Carrier, Alexander Spradlin, John P. Bunce, and Larry D. Rosen. "Virtual Empathy: Positive and Negative Impacts of Going Online upon Empathy in Young Adults."

*Computers in Human Behavior.* Pergamon, June 10, 2015. https://www.sciencedirect.com/science/article/pii/S0747563215003970.

[97]Helen G. M. Vossen,, and Patti M. Valkenburg. "Do Social Media Foster or Curtail Adolescents' Empathy? A Longitudinal Study." Computers in Human Behavior. Pergamon, May 20, 2016. https://www.sciencedirect.com/science/article/pii/S0747563216303673.

[98]Podcast, Kaitlin Luna interviewing Sara Konrath. *Speaking of Psychology,* Episode 95: "The Decline in Empathy and Rise of Narcissism." December 4, 2019. https://www.apa.org/research/action/speaking-of-psychology/empathy-narcissism

[99]Christopher T. Barry, Rebecca L. Kauten, and Joyce H.L. Lui. "Self-Perceptions of Social Support and Empathy as Potential Moderators in the Relation between Adolescent Narcissism and Aggression." Individual Differences Research, 2014. https://www.researchgate.net/profile/Christopher-Barry-5/publication/289541431_Self-perceptions_of_social_support_and_empathy_as_potential_moderators_in_the_relation_between_adolescent_narcissism_and_aggression/links/5693f89a08ae3ad8e33b499e/Self-perceptions-of-social-support-and-empathy-as-potential-moderators-in-the-relation-between-adolescent-narcissism-and-aggression.pdf.

[100]Kaitlin Ugolik Phillips, *The Future of Feeling: Building Empathy in a Tech-Obsessed World.* Amazon Publishing, 2020.

[101]Michael W. Kraus, "Voice-Only Communication Enhances Empathic Accuracy." apa.org. *American Psychologist,* 2017. https://www.apa.org/pubs/journals/releases/amp-amp0000147.pdf.

[102]Karen Dineen Wagner "New Findings About Children's Mental Health During COVID-19." *Psychiatric Times,* October 7, 2020. https://www.psychiatrictimes.com/view/new-findings-children-mental-health-covid-19.

[103]Kalhan Rosenblatt, "Cyberbullying Tragedy: New Jersey Family to Sue After 12-Year-Old Daughter's Suicide." NBCUniversal News Group, August 2, 2017. https://www.nbcnews.com/news/us-news/new-jersey-family-sue-school-district-after-12-year-old-n788506.

## Chapter 7

[104]"All the Latest Cyber Bullying Statistics and What They Mean In 2021." BroadbandSearch.net. Accessed June 4, 2021. https://www.broadbandsearch.net/blog/cyber-bullying-statistics.

[105]"The Annual Bullying Survey 2017." Ditch the Label, 2017. https://www.ditchthelabel.org/wp-content/uploads/2017/07/The-Annual-Bullying-Survey-2017-1.pdf.

[106]Maeve Duggan, "Online Harassment 2017." Pew Research Center: Internet, Science & Tech.Accessed September 18, 2020. https://www.pewresearch.org/internet/2017/07/11/online-harassment-2017/.

[107]Triantoro, Safaria, Fathul Lubabin Nuqul, Eny Purwandari, et al. *International Journal of Scientific and Technology Research:* "The Role of Dark Triad Personality on Cyberbullying: Is It Still a Problem?", February 28, 2020. https://www.semanticscholar.org/

paper/The-Role-Of-Dark-Triad-Personality-On-Is-It-Still-A-Safaria-Nuqul/3008cde-4c69887009a622095f3a4a234e9b69f98.

[108]Mitch van Geel, Anouk Goemans, Fatih Toprak, and Paul Vedder. "Which Personality Traits Are Related to Traditional Bullying and Cyberbullying? A Study with the Big Five, Dark Triad and Sadism." *Personality and Individual Differences*. Pergamon, February 1, 2017. https://www.sciencedirect.com/science/article/abs/pii/S019188691631100X.

[109]Justin W. Patchin,. "Self-Esteem and Cyberbullying." Cyberbullying Research Center, September 24, 2010. https://cyberbullying.org/self-esteem-and-cyberbullying.

[110]Z. K. Fan, Cui-Ying, Xiao-Wei Chu, Meng Zhang, Zong-Kui Zhou. "Are Narcissists More Likely to Be Involved in Cyberbullying? Examining the Mediating Role of Self-Esteem." *Journal of Interpersonal Violence,* August 2019. U.S. National Library of Medicine. Accessed June 4, 2021. https://pubmed.ncbi.nlm.nih.gov/27565705/.

[111]Sherri Gordon, https://www.verywellfamily.com/reasons-why-kids-cyberbully-others-460553. Article accessed at this link is actually "Eight Motives Behind Why Kids Cyberbully" from July 10, 2020, same author.

[112]Charles E. Notar, Sharon Padgett, and Jessica Roden. "Cyberbullying: A Review of the Literature." www.hrpub.org. *Universal Journal of Educational Research,* 2013. https://files.eric.ed.gov/fulltext/EJ1053975.pdf.

[113]"What to Do When Your Child Cyberbullies Others: Top Ten Tips for Parents." Cyberbullying Research Center, October 22, 2020. https://cyberbullying.org/what-to-do-when-your-child-cyberbullies-others.

[114]E. J. Dickson, "Inside the Bright Life of a Murdered Hollywood Sex Therapist." *Rolling Stone,* March 10, 2020.https://www.rollingstone.com/culture/culture-features/amie-harwick-gareth-pursehouse-hollywood-sex-therapist-death-957882/.

[115]Evita March, Verity Litten, Danny H. Sullivan, and Louise Ward. "Somebody That I (Used to) Know: Gender and Dimensions of Dark Personality Traits as Predictors of Intimate Partner Cyberstalking." *Personality and Individual Differences*. Science Direct, September 1, 2020. https://www.sciencedirect.com/science/article/abs/pii/S0191886920302737.

[116]Lily Moor and Joel R. Anderson. "A Systematic Literature Review of the Relationship between Dark Personality Traits and Antisocial Online Behaviours." *Personality and Individual Differences*. Pergamon, March 2, 2019. https://www.sciencedirect.com/science/article/abs/pii/S0191886919301369.

[117]Written by Steve Symanovich for NortonLifeLock: "Cyberstalking: Help Protect Yourself against Cyberstalking." Accessed June 8, 2021. https://us.norton.com/internetsecurity-how-to-how-to-protect-yourself-from-cyberstalkers.html.

[118]Erin E. Buckels, Paul D. Trapnell, and Delroy L. Paulhus. "Trolls Just Want to Have Fun." *Personality and Individual Differences*. Pergamon, February 8, 2014. https://www.sciencedirect.com/science/article/abs/pii/S0191886914000324.

[119]Maria Di Blasi, Alessandro Giardina, Gianluca Lo Coco, et al. "A Compensatory Model to Understand Dysfunctional Personality Traits in Problematic Gaming: The Role of Vulnerable Narcissism." *Personality and Individual Differences*. Pergamon, February 28, 2020. https://www.sciencedirect.com/science/article/abs/pii/S0191886920301100.

[120]Cecilia D'Anastasio, "How 'Roblox' Became a Playground for Virtual

Fascists." *Wired,* June 18, 2020. Accessed July 4, 2021. https://www.wired.com/story/roblox-online-games-irl-fascism-roman-empire/.

[121]Angela Brown. "Predators at Play: How Kids Can Be Targeted through Online Gaming." WCIV, February 11, 2020. https://abcnews4.com/news/local/predators-at-play-how-kids-can-be-targeted-through-online-gaming-02-12-2020.

[122]Graham G. Scott, Stacey Wiencierz, and Christopher J. Hand. "The Volume and Source of Cyberabuse Influences Victim Blame and Perceptions of Attractiveness." *Computers in Human Behavior.* Elsevier, October 31, 2018. https://www.sciencedirect.com/science/article/abs/pii/S0747563218305351?via%3Dihub.

[123]Graham G. Scott, Zara P. Brodie, Megan J. Wilson, et al. "Celebrity Abuse on Twitter: The Impact of Tweet Valence, Volume of Abuse, and Dark Triad Personality Factors on Victim Blaming and Perceptions of Severity." *Computers in Human Behavior.* Elsevier, September 24, 2019. https://www.sciencedirect.com/science/article/abs/pii/S0747563219303462.

[124]Christopher J. Hand,, Graham G. Scott, Zara P. Brodie, Xilei Ye, and Sara C. Sereno. "Tweet Valence, Volume of Abuse, and Observers' Dark Tetrad Personality Factors Influence Victim-Blaming and the Perceived Severity of Twitter Cyberabuse." *Computers in Human Behavior Reports.* Elsevier, January 25, 2021. https://www.sciencedirect.com/science/article/pii/S245195882100004X#bib68.

[125]Dr. Jessica Taylor, *Why Women Are Blamed for Everything: Exploring the Victim-Blaming of Women Subjected to Violence and Trauma.* S.l.: Constable, 2021.

[126]"Author of Book about Victim Blaming Bombarded with Misogynist Abuse." *The Guardian,* April 24, 2020. https://www.theguardian.com/books/2020/apr/24/author-book-victim-blaming-misogynist-abuse-jessica-taylor.

[127]*American Murder: The Family Next Door.* Netflix, 2020.

[128]Scott W. Keiller, "Male Narcissism and Attitudes Toward Heterosexual Women and Men, Lesbian Women, and Gay Men: Hostility toward Heterosexual Women Most of All." Open Access Kent State (OAKS), February 23, 2015. https://oaks.kent.edu/psycpubs/57.

[129]"Narcissistic Men Typically Direct Their Rage at Straight Women." MedicineNet, August 9, 2010. https://www.medicinenet.com/script/main/art.asp?articlekey=118736.

[130]Mark Follman, "Armed and Misogynist: How Toxic Masculinity Fuels Mass Shootings." *Mother Jones,* May/June 2019. https://www.motherjones.com/crime-justice/2019/06/domestic-violence-misogyny-incels-mass-shootings/.

## Chapter 8

[131]Mary L. Trump, *Too Much and Never Enough: How My Family Created the World's Most Dangerous Man.* S.l.: Simon & Schuster Ltd., 2021.

[132]Jerrold M. Post, Narcissism and *Politics: Dreams of Glory.* New York, NY: Cambridge University Press, 2015.

[133]Stanton Peele, "Edwards' Confession Shows Us Just How Nutty and Narcissistic He Is." *Psychology Today.* Sussex Publishers. August 10, 2008, accessed June 10, 2021. https://www.psychologytoday.com/us/blog/addiction-in-society/200808/edwards-confession-shows-us-just-how-nutty-and-narcissistic-he-is.

[134]Rich Morin, "The Most Narcissistic U.S. Presidents." Pew Research Center, November

14, 2013, accessed May 30, 2020. https://www.pewresearch.org/fact-tank/2013/11/14/
the-most-narcissistic-u-s-presidents/.

[135]Boris Duspara and Tobias Greitemeyer. "The Impact of Dark Tetrad Traits on Political
Orientation and Extremism: An Analysis in the Course of a Presidential Election." Heliyon.
Elsevier, October 10, 2017. https://www.ncbi.nlm.nih.gov/pmc/articles/PMC5680983/.

[136]Peter K. Hatemi, and Zoltán Fazekas. "Narcissism and Political Orientations." American
Journal of Political Science, Wiley Online Library. John Wiley & Sons, Ltd, July 14, 2018.
https://onlinelibrary.wiley.com/doi/abs/10.1111/ajps.12380.

[137]Sabrina J. Mayer, Carl C. Berning, and David Johann. "The Two Dimensions of Narcissistic Personality and Support for the Radical Right: The Role of Right-Wing Authoritarianism, Social Dominance Orientation and Anti-immigrant Sentiment." European Journal
of Personality, Wiley Online Library. John Wiley & Sons, Ltd, January 9, 2020. https://
onlinelibrary.wiley.com/doi/full/10.1002/per.2228.

[138]Eric W. Dolan, "Narcissistic Rivalry Indirectly Linked to Support for Radical Right Populism, According to New Psychology Study." PsyPost, January 16, 2020. https://www.psypost.
org/2020/01/narcissistic-rivalry-indirectly-linked-to-support-for-radical-right-popu-
lism-according-to-new-psychology-study-55256.

[139]Cameron S. Kay, "Actors of the Most Fiendish Character: Explaining the Associations
between the Dark Tetrad and Conspiracist Ideation." Personality and Individual Differences. Pergamon, March 2021. https://www.sciencedirect.com/science/article/abs/pii/
S0191886920307340.

[140]Beth Elwood, "New Psychology Research Uncovers Why People with 'Dark Tetrad'
Personality Traits Are More Likely to Believe Conspiracy Theories." PsyPost, June 8,
2021. https://www.psypost.org/2021/06/new-psychology-research-uncovers-why-peo-
ple-with-dark-tetrad-personality-traits-are-more-likely-to-believe-conspiracy-theo-
ries-61088.

[141]"New Perspectives: The Way Out." Jigsaw. Google. Accessed June 13, 2021. https://jigsaw.
google.com/the-current/white-supremacy/new-perspectives/.

[142]Sandeep Roy, Craig S. Neumann, Daniel N. Jones, et al. "Psychopathic Propensities
Contribute to Social Dominance Orientation and Right-Wing Authoritarianism in Pre-
dicting Prejudicial Attitudes in a Large European Sample." Personality and Individual
Differences. Pergamon, January 2021. https://www.sciencedirect.com/science/article/abs/
pii/S0191886920305468?via%3Dihub.

[143]"Follow the Leader: Narcissists Tend to Gravitate toward Trump." Union College
News and Events, October 27, 2020. https://www.union.edu/news/stories/202010/
follow-leader-narcissists-tend-gravitate-toward-trump.

[144]Cyber racism. Semantic Scholar. (n.d.). Retrieved February 11, 2022, from https://www.
semanticscholar.org/topic/Cyber-racism/2280539

[145]Golec de Zavala, A., Dyduch-Hazar, K., & Lantos, D. (2019, February). Collective narcissism: Political consequences of investing self worth in the ingroup's image. American
Psychological Association. Retrieved February 11, 2022, from https://psycnet.apa.org/
record/2019-16213-002

[146]Scott Simon, and Emma Bowman. "How One Mom Talks to Her Sons About Hate on the Internet." NPR, August 17, 2019. https://www.npr.org/2019/08/17/751986787writer-joanna-schroeder-on-preventing-teenage-boys-from-turning-to-hate.

[147]Brendesha M. Tynes, "Online Racial Discrimination: A Growing Problem for Adolescents." *Psychological Science Agenda,* December 2015. American Psychological Association. Accessed June 13, 2021. https://www.apa.org/science/about/psa/2015/12/online-racial-discrimination.

[148]Lieberman, B. M., Lieberman, M., Lieberman, M. L. M., Jones, T., Glader, P., Tompkins, A., O'Rourke, C., & Edmonds, R. (2021, November 16). *A growing group of journalists has cut back on Twitter, or abandoned it entirely.* Poynter. Retrieved February 11, 2022, from https://www.poynter.org/reporting-editing/2021/a-growing-group-of-journalists-has-cut-back-on-twitter-or-abandoned-it-entirely/

[149]"Troll Patrol Findings." *Troll Patrol Report.* Accessed June 13, 2021. https://decoders.amnesty.org/projects/troll-patrol/findings.

[150]Shoshana Zuboff. *The Age of Surveillance Capitalism: The Fight for the Future at the New Frontier of Power.* London: Profile Books, 2019.

[151]Donell Holloway, "Explainer: What Is Surveillance Capitalism and How Does It Shape Our Economy?" The Conversation, June 24, 2019. https://theconversation.com/explainer-what-is-surveillance-capitalism-and-how-does-it-shape-our-economy-119158.

[152]Shoshana Zuboff, "The Threat of Surveillance Capitalism, and the Fight for a Human Future." ABC Religion & Ethics. Australian Broadcasting Corporation, August 21, 2019. https://www.abc.net.au/religion/shoshana-zuboff-threat-of-surveillance-capitalism/11433716.

[153]Janice Gassam Asare, "Social Media Continues to Amplify White Supremacy and Suppress Anti-Racism." *Forbes Magazine,* January 9, 2021. https://www.forbes.com/sites/janicegassam/2021/01/08/social-media-continues-to-amplify-white-supremacy-and-suppress-anti-racism/?sh=3168d4424170.

[154]Nadeem, R. (2021, May 19). *Silencing Palestinian voices in the Digital age.* Digital Rights Monitor. Retrieved February 11, 2022, from https://www.digitalrightsmonitor.pk/suppressing-palestinian-voices-in-the-digital-age/

[155]Donna Tam, "Social Media Censorship from Around the World." Marketplace, April 29, 2019. https://www.marketplace.org/2016/05/27/social-media-censorship-around-world/.

[156]Editorial. "The Times and Iraq." *New York Times,* May 26, 2004. https://www.nytimes.com/2004/05/26/world/from-the-editors-the-times-and-iraq.html.

[157]Steve Rathje, Jay J. Van Bavel, and Sander van der Linden. "Out-Group Animosity Drives Engagement on Social Media." Proceedings of the National Academy of Sciences (PNAS), June 29, 2021. https://www.pnas.org/content/118/26/e2024292118.

[158]Gabriel Geiger, "Norway Law Forces Influencers to Label Retouched Photos on Instagram." VICE. June 29, 2021; accessed August 2, 2021. https://www.vice.com/en/article/g5gd99norway-law-forces-influencers-to-label-etouched-photos-on-instagram.

## Chapter 9

[159]Eric Johnson, "If You Can Quit Social Media, but Don't, Then You're Part of the Problem, Jaron Lanier Says." Vox, July 27, 2018. https://www.vox.com/2018/7/27/17618756/jaron-lanier-deleting-social-media-book-kara-swisher-too-embarrassed-podcast.